SHE CHOSE TO RISE

A Global Rise & Soar Publication

SHE CHOSE TO RISE

Stories of Women Who Refused to Stay Down

Edited by

Mariatu Esther Kabba

Publisher line at bottom:

Global Rise & Soar
Phoenix, Arizona & Freetown, Sierra Leone

The stories in this book are personal narratives written by individual contributors. Each story reflects the author's personal experience and perspective.

Published by Global Rise & Soar
Phoenix, Arizona & Freetown, Sierra Leone
ISBN: 978-1-972325-07-0
First Edition
Cover design: Natasa Ivancevic
Interior design: weformatbook.com
Book Publishing Consultant: www.serapisbeypublishing.com

For more information:
info@globalriseandsoar.com
globalriseandsoar.com

Dedication

For every woman who ever thought her voice didn't matter may these stories remind you that rising is your birthright. For my mother, who showed me that survival is sacred and that Sierra Leonean women carry nations on their backs.

This book exists because you never stopped believing.

Epigraph

"Each time a woman stands up for herself, she stands up for all women."

— Maya Angelou

Table of Contents

Introduction: When Women Rise, The World Transforms

By Mariatu Esther Kabba

This book began as a whisper in my spirit.

I was sitting in my small office in Freetown, Sierra Leone, working on yet another radio program about women's rights, when I felt God place a question in my heart: What if women from across the world could speak to each other, across borders, languages, and cultures, and discover they are not alone?

That whisper became a vision. And that vision became She Chose to Rise.

I am Mariatu Esther Kabba, and I carry my own story of rising. I grew up in Freetown, Sierra Leone, the daughter of a civil servant who died when I was six years old. His death shattered our family's stability and our sense of belonging. My mother—stripped of her husband's protection in a society that views widows and their daughters as less than—had to start over with nothing.

I know what it feels like to be dismissed, to go to bed hungry, to fight for an education that others take for granted. I know what it means to sleep on a church floor because you chose your voice over a roof. I know the cost of speaking when silence feels safer.

And I know what it means to rise anyway.

For over a decade, I have worked in media development and women's empowerment across Africa. I trained more than 200 journalists through the BBC Media Action Girls' Education and Empowerment Project. I founded Hope Pathways Global (formerly Strong Women, Strong Girls Sierra Leone) to mentor young women in rural communities who, like me, needed someone to believe in them. In 2021, I was honored as one of Sierra Leone's Fifty Most Influential Women and received the Mandela Washington YALI Fellowship. In 2023, I was awarded the Fulbright Hubert Humphrey Fellowship.

But this book is not about my achievements. It is about what I have learned through every woman I have met, every story I have heard, every community I have served: women across the world are fighting the same battles, carrying the same wounds, and discovering the same truth—that rising is not a privilege, it is a choice.

Why These Women, Why Now

When I put out the call for women to share their stories for this project, I didn't know who would respond. I knew only that I wanted voices that represented the fullness of our global sisterhood—different cultures, different faiths, different struggles, but one shared heartbeat.

Six women answered.

From Bangladesh to Brazil. From Albania to Djibouti. From Ukraine and the United States to my own Sierra Leone.

Some are Muslims. Some are Christians. Some found faith in the middle of crisis. Some are still searching. Some faced war. Some faced illness. Some faced systems designed to silence them. All of them faced a moment when they had to decide: Will I stay down, or will I rise?

These are not stories of women who were born brave. These are stories of women who were terrified—and chose courage anyway.

And as I curated their stories, I realized something: My story belongs here too.

Not because I'm the editor. But because I, too, had a moment when I had to choose. A night when I chose my voice over shelter. A cold church floor where I learned that rising isn't about comfort, it's about the moment when staying small becomes more unbearable than the risk of standing tall.

So in these pages, you'll find seven women—six whose stories I gathered, and one (mine) that I couldn't tell in full without losing the thread of what this anthology is meant to be: a collection of defining moments, not complete life stories.

My full journey—from that church floor to training hundreds of journalists, from being called "mad" like my mother to being named one of Sierra Leone's Most Influential Women will be told in my forthcoming memoir. But the moment that changed everything? That's here, alongside these remarkable women.

What This Book Is—And What It Is Not

This is not a book of easy inspiration or Instagram-worthy quotes. These stories are raw, real, and sometimes painful to read.

You will meet Elita, who stood frozen as her stalker followed her for months—until the day she locked him in a music shop and finally said, "Enough."

You will meet Zineb, the girl who had sand poured on her head and learned that beauty standards are nothing more than history and geography written on our bodies.

You will meet me, Mariatu, on the night I chose my voice over shelter and learned that a fatherless daughter from Sierra Leone had nothing left to lose—and everything to prove.

You will meet Elira, who grew up under communism, became a journalist during her country's fragile new democracy, and fought to prove that a woman can be both a mother and a leader without having to choose.

You will meet Olga, who woke to explosions at 3:40 a.m. as her country went to war—and learned that courage is choosing to live fully even when the sirens are still sounding.

You will meet Marianna, who built a successful career, lost herself to burnout, faced breast cancer, and discovered that sometimes rising means starting completely over at forty.

You will meet Dr. Adelaida, who was told she didn't have "the look" for television, who built a business with her husband, who buried him after thirty-three years of marriage—and who distilled her life into five powerful F-words that guide her still.

And after each story, you will hear from me again, not as a contributor, but as an editor reflecting on what these women taught me. These brief reflections are my way of showing you why I chose each story, what it revealed to me, and how it connects to the next woman's journey.

Because that's what this anthology is: a conversation. A chorus of voices speaking across borders, saying the same thing in different languages: We chose to rise. And so can you.

This Is Bigger Than a Book

She Chose to Rise is not just a collection of stories. It is the foundation of a movement.

I created this project under the umbrella of Global Rise & Soar, a platform dedicated to impactful storytelling, transformational leadership, and global empowerment. My vision is to build a space where women across the world can share their truths, heal from their wounds, and step into their God-given purpose.

This book is the beginning.

After this, there will be a podcast where these women's voices come alive in conversation. There will be live events where their stories are told on stage. There will be workshops, summits, and gatherings where women from every corner of the globe discover they are part of something larger than themselves.

I am building this because I believe that when women rise, everything changes. Families change. Communities change. Nations change.

And I am building this because I know, deep in my bones, that there are women reading these words right now who need to know: You are not alone. Your pain has purpose. Your story matters.

How to Read This Book

I have organized these stories into three parts, each reflecting a stage in the journey of rising:

Part One and Two: Breaking and Rebuilding- Stories of women who were broken by violence, culture, loss, or systems designed to silence them—and who chose to rebuild themselves on their own terms. Here you'll find the majority of our stories: moments of shattering, of choosing, of discovering that the rubble can become a foundation.

Part Three: Living in Your Power- the story of a woman who has learned to define success on her own terms, who has faced the deepest loss, and who now lights the way for others. This section is intentionally smaller, not because there are fewer stories of triumph, but because most of life is spent in the breaking and rebuilding. The "arrived" moments are rare, brief, and still complicated.

You can read this book from beginning to end, or you can open it to the story that calls to you. You can read it alone, or with your book club, your church group, your circle of friends.

However you read it, I invite you to do so with an open heart.

These women have trusted us with their truths. The least we can do is honor them by receiving their stories with the tenderness and courage they deserve.

A Personal Invitation

If you are reading this and you are in your own season of rising—whether you are just learning to stand, or you have been standing so long you forgot how to rest, I want you to know something:

This book is for you.

These women wrote their stories so that you would know you are not crazy, not broken, not too much or not enough.

You are in the process of becoming. And becoming is never a straight line. It is messy, painful, beautiful, and sacred. So, take what you need from these pages. Let their courage become your courage. Let their voices become a chorus that drowns out the lies you've been told about who you are and what you're worth.

And when you are ready, when your own moment of rising comes—I pray you will choose it.

Because the world is waiting for you. And we need you to rise.

With love and faith,
Mariatu Esther Kabba
Lead Consultant, Global Rise & Soar LLC
Founder & Executive Director, Hope Pathways Global Inc
Phoenix, Arizona & Freetown, Sierra Leone
November 2025

Editor's Note: My full story—from that church floor to the fellowships, the organizations, and the movement—will be told in my forthcoming memoir. What you'll find in these pages is the moment that made everything else possible: the night I chose my voice.

PART ONE

BREAKING THE SILENCE

Introduction

Silence is not always golden. Sometimes it's a cage.

The three women whose stories open this collection know this truth intimately. They lived in worlds where speaking up could cost them everything—their safety, their dignity, their place in society. And yet, each of them reached a moment where silence became more dangerous than speaking.

In Bangladesh, a young woman stood frozen under mockery and harassment until the day she walked into a music shop and locked the door behind her stalker. In Tunisia, a girl with curly hair absorbed cruelty about her appearance until she understood that beauty standards were nothing more than geography and history written on her body. In Sierra Leone, a daughter who lost her father and her home learned that when institutions fail you, your voice becomes your most powerful tool.

These are not stories about women who were naturally brave. These are stories about women who were afraid—and spoke anyway.

Because sometimes, rising begins with a single word: No

The Day I Stopped Running

By Elita Karim, Musician, Bangladesh

When I was in my late teens, I had a stalker who followed me to university every morning. Early mornings were the scariest. The streets were emptier, and my cycle rickshaw moved slowly along the narrow roads of Dhaka. His car – powerful and loud – would slide up beside me and match my pace. Sometimes he would roll down the window and make comments, sharp catcalls that pierced through the silence. Sometimes he would drive ahead, park in front of my rickshaw, and slow me down intentionally, like a predator enjoying his chase. This went on for weeks. Then months. Soon, my 8 a.m. classes filled me with dread. I started missing lectures. I didn't tell anyone.

I was a young woman in a society where a woman's misfortune is almost always blamed on her. I could already hear the questions: What were you wearing? Did you look at him? Maybe you smiled? Maybe you liked the attention?

I refused to play that victim-blaming game.

But silence has a cost.

Every day, fear hollowed me out a little more. My grades slipped. My laughter grew quieter. I started to disappear from my own life. Back in the early to mid-2000s, talking about mental health wasn't normal.

Words like "depression" were whispered, if spoken at all. People believed that if you had food, family, and education, you had no right to feel sad.

I was scared – not just of my stalker, but of my society. I didn't want to seem weak. I didn't want to be pitied. I didn't want to be the "girl with a problem." Looking back now, I realize I should have sought professional help or at least confided in someone. But at that time, I didn't even have the vocabulary to describe what I was going through. Fear had no language. It just sat inside me, heavy and unrelenting.

The Moment Everything Changed

One afternoon, exhausted from pretending everything was fine, I overheard my mother speaking to her sister on the phone. She was offering comfort over something unrelated, but her voice carried strength and certainty. "No matter what happens," she said, "I am there to support my children and the people I love."

Those words were meant for someone else, but they reached a part of me I thought was numb. I realized then that if I ever fell into a pit so deep and shameful that society would rather bury me than help me, my mother would still stand by me.

I don't know why I felt that assurance. I never told her about the stalking. Maybe, at that age, I saw family and society as one and the same – and I had grown to distrust both. But that evening, something shifted.

One day, as I crossed the busy road toward my university building, I saw him again. He was outside his car this time, standing at a distance, watching me. Waiting. Something inside me snapped – not in fear, but in resolve. Across the street was a small music store I often visited. It sold CDs, DVDs, and pirated movies – a haven for students hungry for art in the pre-streaming days.

I walked straight in.

My stalker followed, just as I knew he would.

What he didn't know was that I had spoken to the store owner earlier that week. I had asked for his help if the man ever followed me inside. The owner had agreed, kind and fatherly in his quiet way.

As soon as the stalker entered, the owner locked the door.

The Confrontation. The shop was nearly empty – just two staff members and a few students searching for the latest Harry Potter DVD. I turned toward the man who had been haunting me for months. My voice shook at first but then grew louder, carried by months of buried rage. "What do you want from me?" I shouted.

"Why are you following me? Why do you stop my rickshaw? Why do you throw paper notes asking me to run away with you? What kind of man does this?" I was trembling, crying, screaming – but I didn't stop. My pain, my humiliation, my exhaustion poured out like a storm that refused to end.

The man froze, startled by my sudden defiance. He tried to run, but the locked door stopped him. The students turned toward us, alert. The shop owner raised his voice: "There's a CCTV camera. Everything is being recorded."

In the early 2000s in Bangladesh, that sentence carried weight – CCTV cameras were rare, powerful witnesses.

Cornered, the man lashed out with venom. "She asked for it! She led me on! Look at her – she loves attention! She's a whore!"

For a second, my heart sank. This was my biggest fear – that even in this moment of courage, people would believe him. That society would once again side with the predator. I almost turned to run toward the back door, to escape the shame that was flooding back. But then, something remarkable happened.

The young students browsing DVDs stepped forward. One of them, barely older than me, said calmly, "You have no right to talk to her like that. Apologise." Another added, "We're calling the police."

The man's face was drained of color. He stammered, "No, please…"

The students didn't move. "You have no right to accuse her. She has every right to walk these streets. This is her city too."

When the owner finally unlocked the door, the stalker fled.

For the first time in months, I breathed freely.

My hands still shook, but they were shaking with relief, not fear.

What I Learned

Word of the incident spread through my small private university. What surprised me most was not the gossip, but the support.

Professors checked in on me. Students whispered words of encouragement. Others came forward with their own stories – of fear, harassment, silence. Some told me they had always believed speaking out was pointless, but after that day, they weren't so sure anymore.

I realized then that courage is contagious. One voice trembling in fear can awaken others. That incident didn't make me fearless overnight. But it changed something fundamental in me.

I learned that silence protects no one – not the victim, not the next girl, not the community. When I chose to speak, I wasn't just defending myself; I was reclaiming the space that fear had taken away.

It also taught me that strength can come from unexpected places. I couldn't find refuge in institutions or family conversations – but I found it in music, in the kindness of strangers, in the solidarity of young people who refused to look away. Maybe that's why music has always been my savior – the rhythm that steadies me, the melody that reminds me that I survived.

Years later, I often revisit that moment in my mind – the dusty sunlight spilling through the glass door of the music shop, my trembling voice cutting through the air, the stunned silence before others chose to act. That was the day I stopped running.

A Message to Every Woman

If I could speak to that young woman now, I would tell her this:

Fear is a liar.

Shame is a thief.

And silence is their weapon.

I would tell her that it's okay to ask for help, to cry, to shout, to seek therapy, to speak truth even when your voice shakes. I would tell her that society's rules are written in pencil – and we all have the right to erase and rewrite them.

To every woman who has been followed, silenced, dismissed, or doubted – I hope you remember this:

You do not owe the world your silence. You owe yourself your peace. Sometimes, rising doesn't mean conquering mountains or winning wars. Sometimes, rising means walking into a music store, locking a door, and finally saying the words that have been trapped inside you for too long. That day, I learned that courage doesn't always roar. Sometimes courage is the quiet voice at the end of the day saying, "I will try again tomorrow."

Sometimes it's the voice that simply says, "Enough."

> "Courage doesn't always roar. Sometimes courage is the quiet voice at the end of the day saying, I will try again tomorrow."
>
> – Mary Anne Radmacher

Transition

Elita's confrontation in the music shop was a single afternoon that changed the course of her life. But for some women, the silencing begins so early that it shapes the very foundation of who they believe they can become. Zineb's story takes us back to childhood—to a Sunday afternoon when sand was poured on a little girl's head, and the long journey it took to shake it off.

What This Story Taught Me
Mariatu Esther Kabba, Editor

When Elita first shared her story with me, I asked her: "Were you scared the whole time?"

Her answer surprised me: "I was scared. But I was also tired. And being tired of being scared is its own kind of bravery."

This is what Elita's story teaches us: Courage isn't the absence of fear. Courage is the moment when you realize that continuing to be afraid is more exhausting than facing the thing you're afraid of. For months, Elita lived in paralyzing fear, rearranging her life, changing her routes, looking over her shoulder. The fear consumed more energy than action would have. And when she finally acted, when she locked him in that music shop and called the police, it wasn't because she suddenly felt brave. It was because she was simply too tired to keep running.

I see this pattern in women's stories everywhere. We endure, we accommodate, we adjust, we shrink, until one day, the cost of staying small becomes greater than the risk of standing tall. That's when we rise. Not because we're fearless, but because we're exhausted by fear.

Elita's story also reminds us that stalking, harassment, and violence against women are normalized in ways that protect perpetrators and shame victims. For months, people told Elita she was overreacting, being dramatic, taking it too seriously. This is how predators thrive—through our collective gaslighting of women's danger perception.

Women know when they're not safe. We need to trust them.

As you move to the next story, you'll meet Zineb—a woman who learned that the standards used to measure our worth are just as arbitrary as the fears others try to impose on us.

The Girl Who Stood Still Under the Sand

By Zineb Haddaji, Documentary photographer, Djiboutian

Sunday was the worst day of the week for me: bath day.

From the morning, my mother would scrub my body and wash my hair without styling it, leaving it fluffy until it dried, then making braids for me in the evening. I would go out to play with the neighborhood children who never stopped mocking me while I hid my anger and tears under my hair, which sat on my head like a poorly made umbrella. Suddenly, a handful of sand from the garden was poured on top of my head.

The sand seeped slowly from above my hair, and some of it got stuck between my curly locks. I was frozen in place from the shock. The girls around me were laughing, and their voices violently invaded my ears like chisels. This happened in the neighborhood square on a Sunday while I was playing when I was eight years old. I didn't know what to do then: should I go back home for my mother to punish me, or stay there and endure the children's laughter? I cried for a long time under the wall of the public garden and returned home at sunset. When I told my mother what happened, prepared for punishment, she was about to scold me—but then I burst into tears. She hugged me tightly and said, "It's okay, we'll wash it again. Don't cry, my dear."

I cannot deny that this lightened the weight of what happened, but it didn't make me forget it.

Learning What Beauty Means

This incident made me aware early on of so-called beauty standards.

Why is the white girl with long silky hair considered the most beautiful? Why are we not equal in society's eyes? How does appearance affect my opportunities and chances in life? Am I so ugly that I deserve to be bullied and mocked?

The older I got, the more I felt different and the greater my sense that I was incapable of fitting into any group. In adolescence, my friends' complexions changed and their feminine features emerged, but that didn't happen with me. I remained thin with curly hair—"Somali," as they called me in my city in southern Tunisia.

This worried my parents. They would complain that I was an overly sensitive child. Sometimes my mother would lose patience with the long crying spells that would overcome me when someone hurt me with a harsh comment about my appearance. She didn't understand what bothered me and would say, "You are so ungrateful. You are a spoiled child. We provide you with everything: clothes, education, food and drink. What more do you want from life than this?"

Unfortunately, my mother is a woman who did not receive advanced education. She was forced to leave school to take care of household matters after her older sister got married early. All of this did not help her understand her daughter—me, a very sensitive child who asked difficult questions and thought deeply about myself and what was happening around me.

I felt alienated day after day.

I was constantly anxious and full of worries about the future. How long will I remain like this—unaccepted and misunderstood by everyone? The place felt suffocating. Nothing made me happy. I worked harder than necessary in my studies and in everything I did to please others, but I still didn't see any light at the end of the tunnel.

Finding Myself in Books

The state of psychological confusion and search for identity pushed me toward reading.

Reading became my ideal means to escape from the reality surrounding me. I would spend long summer vacation days with novels, living with their characters for days at a time. Reading literature taught me to care more about the hidden depths of the human self, which pushed me toward other genres: history, philosophy, sociology, anthropology, political science.

I'm not exaggerating when I say that reading was a lifeline for me and still is.

It taught me how to understand and deconstruct the things around me. I understood that I am different and that my appearance is the result of geography and history that shaped southern Tunisia. With it came stereotypical beauty standards and racist behavior—remnants of the centuries-old trade routes linking Europe, Africa, and the Americas. This body through which I exist in this world is a descendant of all these events.

After this phase of understanding, I got involved in volunteer and community work. I was elected president of the municipal children's council in the governorate of Medenine in southern Tunisia when I was thirteen years old. That was a turning point in my life—the first time I was able to practice leadership in my small environment.

I began to gradually free myself from the stereotypical beauty standards that weighed on my self-confidence. It was a great challenge for a young teenager.

I took my mission as president of the children's municipality very seriously. I tried to do my work to the fullest despite the pressures I was subjected to. My father's work as a police officer under Ben Ali's dictatorial regime made fear follow me everywhere. I would measure my words in public and private spaces. My father was the sole provider for our family, including my grandfather, grandmother, and aunts.

When I knew that my life in Tunisia had become almost impossible, I decided to emigrate.

The Land Where My Face Was Familiar

I got a job opportunity in Djibouti. I packed a suitcase with some clothes and $300 that my father borrowed from a friend, and I left without shedding a single tear. I left open to a new life.

Some accused me of being crazy because Djibouti is not the land of dreams for them, and very few people know of its existence on the planet. But for me it was—and still is—the land of dreams because it embraced me with all its love without asking me about the past.

I quickly integrated among the people, and my face, which was strange in Tunisia, became a familiar face in Djibouti because of my strong resemblance to its inhabitants.

I felt that I was becoming stronger day by day. I wasn't afraid of change. I started a new life from scratch. I made friendships and developed professionally after I resigned from my first job following harassment and disrespect there.

I fell in love and got married in the way that represents me. I had my marriage contract on the weekend: no parties, no white dress, no guests. My conservative family didn't like that and got angry with me, but I am happy and convinced of my decision because for the first time I pleased myself and didn't please others.

I gained greater confidence in myself and no longer cared much about people's opinions. I even stopped straightening my hair with chemicals and let my curly locks embrace the air and enjoy freedom.

Now, I look proudly at my face in the mirror and go out to the street without makeup when I want to.

The Woman I Became

That constantly crying and anxious child became a strong woman.

I began to live according to my convictions and shape my identity based on the experience I accumulated in life. I learned to say no when necessary. And I learned not to cling to what does not resemble me.

Through my humble experience in life, I want to say to every girl who has been subjected to rejection or bullying because of her appearance:

Do not listen to those discouraging voices, for they are nothing but dissonance in the music of life.

Don't let them reduce your existence in this world to merely being a body and nothing more.

Learn. Travel. Embrace yourself with all love. Give yourself time to grow.

Failure is a school where we learn success. Even if you suffer from rejection, don't let that affect your spirit.

Extend a helping hand to those who need it when you are able to do so. Giving makes you a stronger woman with greater influence in her surroundings. Giving is an umbrella that protects you from life's misfortunes. Speaking of umbrellas, I mentioned at the beginning that the children compared my head to a poorly made umbrella when I was little. Yes, my head is an umbrella.

But one so well-made that it deflects hurtful words and bullying away from me.

Transition

Zineb found freedom by leaving—by packing a suitcase and $300 and choosing a new country where her face was finally familiar. But not every woman can leave. Some must fight for change exactly where they are, in systems designed to keep them small. Next, my story Mariatu's story shows us what happens when a woman refuses to accept that poverty, gender, or circumstance will write the ending of her story.

What This Story Taught Me
Mariatu Esther Kabba, Editor

"Beauty standards are just history and geography written on our bodies."

When Zineb said this, something clicked for me.

All those years I was told a "Mandingo girl is not meant for offices," I internalized that as truth about ME. But it was just someone else's limited imagination. It was history (the roles women had always played) and geography (the culture I was born into) trying to write itself onto my body, my voice, my future.

Zineb stood still under that sand, feeling the weight of other people's expectations literally poured onto her head and learned something profound: The things people use to diminish us often say more about their limitations than our worth.

What struck me most about Zineb's story is her refusal to hate the people who hurt her. She recognized that they, too, were operating within systems they didn't create. The aunties who poured sand on her head weren't villains—they were enforcers of a beauty standard they themselves had been subjected to. They were passing down what had been done to them.

This doesn't excuse the harm. But it does reveal something important: When we challenge the standards imposed on us, we're not just freeing ourselves. We're interrupting a cycle. We're refusing to pass down the same limitations to the next generation.

Zineb chose to see beauty as broader, deeper, and more generous than what her culture prescribed. And in doing so, she gave permission to other girls to do the same.

The next woman you'll meet—Elira—also had to redefine what others told her she could or couldn't be.

The Night I Chose My Voice

By Mariatu Esther Kabba

The church floor was cold.

Even through the thin mat I'd laid down, I could feel the hardness of the concrete pressing into my hip, my shoulder, the side of my face. It was my third night sleeping there, and my body still hadn't adjusted. Every position made something ache.

Outside, Freetown was settling into its familiar nighttime rhythm. Generators humming. Vendors calling out final sales. The distant sound of highlife music drifting from someone's radio. Inside the small Pentecostal church on Campbell Street, there was only silence. The smell of old wood. Kerosene. Rain.

I pulled my thin blanket tighter and stared at the ceiling. Two days ago, I'd had a roof. Two days ago, I'd made a choice. I grew up understanding that fatherless daughters in Sierra Leone are question marks. Incomplete. Negotiable.

When my father died, I was six. When my mother, stripped of protection, dismissed as "mad"—could no longer keep me, I was taken by an aunt who meant well but struggled with demons of her own. I moved through homes where I was guest, not family. Where I fetched water at 2 a.m. Where I was reminded, with every misstep, that I carried my mother's brokenness in my blood.

"Your mother's madness is in you." I learned early: Don't expect too much. Be grateful for what you get. Make yourself useful. Stay small.

And I did. Until I couldn't anymore.

By the time I enrolled at Fourah Bay College to study Mass Communications, I'd learned how to survive. How to stretch one uniform across years. How to sell shawarma at school to pay my own fees. How to pretend everything was fine when it wasn't.

But when the college radio station needed volunteers, something inside me said yes before my fear could say no.

I started reading the news. And for the first time in my life, I felt like I was doing what I was made for. My voice, the one I'd been told didn't belong in offices, the one people said was "too much" for a Mandingo girl, carried across airwaves. It informed people. It mattered.

But radio work meant late evenings. It meant missing household chores. It meant prioritizing something I wanted over what was expected of me.

The tension built slowly, then all at once. One morning, I was given a choice. Not with words. Not gently. But clearly. Stop the radio work and stay in the house. Or continue—and leave. I kept going to the station.

On Wednesday, May 13, 2015, it rained. Hard, relentless rain that turned Freetown's streets into rivers of red mud. That evening, I returned home late from the radio station. My clothes were damp. My bag was heavy. I was exhausted.

She was waiting. "You were told to stop."

"I—"

"You think you are too important now? Too good for this house?"

I wanted to explain. I wanted to say that the radio wasn't rebellion, it was survival. That finding my voice felt like finding oxygen after years of holding my breath.

But the words stuck. What came instead was the beating. Sharp. Fast. My cheek stinging. My lips swelling. And then, the words I'd been braced for but somehow wasn't ready to hear:

"Pack your things. Leave." This time, I didn't apologize. I didn't beg to stay. I didn't shrink.

Something had shifted. Maybe it was all those years of being told I was less than finally cracking open. Maybe it was God. Maybe it was just exhaustion from pretending I could keep making myself smaller to fit into spaces that were never built for me.

I packed. And I stepped out into the rain. I had nowhere to go. No family to call. No friends with extra space. No money for a room. Just faith.

And a church I'd passed a hundred times on Campbell Street.

I walked through the rain, my bag on my shoulder, my heart pounding, my feet moving even though I didn't know where I was going, and I prayed.

God, you see me. You know my life. You know my journey. I have nowhere else to go. So I choose you. Lead me.

When I reached the church, the doors were unlocked. I walked in. I laid my mat on the floor. And I stayed. The first night, I cried. The second night, I was numb. By the third night, I was just cold. I lay on that concrete floor, listening to the sounds of a city that had no idea I existed, and I thought about all the times I'd been told to be quiet. To be grateful. To accept my place.

And I thought about my voice. The one that people said didn't belong. The one that carried across radio waves and reached people I'd never meet. The one I'd chosen over a roof.

Was I crazy? Maybe. But I knew something that the people who called me crazy didn't: A fatherless daughter from Freetown had already lost everything that mattered. What was a roof compared to losing myself?

On that third night, lying on the cold floor of a church with nowhere else to go, I prayed again. But this time, it wasn't a plea. It was a surrender.

God, I don't know what happens next. I don't know where I'll sleep tomorrow or how I'll eat or if anyone will ever believe in me. But I know I can't go back to being silent. I can't go back to making myself small. So if this is what choosing my voice costs—then I choose it. Lead me. I'm yours.

And in that moment, something broke open. Not the circumstances. The floor was still cold. The future was still uncertain. I was still alone. But something inside me settled. I had made a choice.

Not once. But over and over, in a thousand small moments leading up to this one. And I would keep making it. What I didn't know that night was that this moment, this cold, terrifying, faithful moment, was the beginning of everything. I didn't know that I would find foster parents who would call me "daughter" without pity.

I didn't know that I would graduate, build organizations, train hundreds of journalists, stand on international stages. I didn't know that one day, I would sit down to write this story, not as a victim, but as a woman who chose her voice and built a life around that choice.

All I knew was this: I was cold. I was scared. I was alone. But I was free. The rain stopped sometime before dawn. When I woke, light was filtering through the church windows, soft and golden. I rolled up my mat. I picked up my bag. And I walked out into a world that hadn't changed, but I had.

People ask me now: Was it worth it? Losing the roof? Sleeping on that floor? Walking away from safety? And I tell them the truth: That night, I learned something no classroom could teach me.

I learned that rising isn't about comfort. It's about choice. And sometimes, the most courageous thing you can do is choose yourself, even when the cost is everything you have.

I chose my voice that night. And my voice chose me back. Everything else followed.

*Mariatu Esther Kabba's full memoir will be published in end of 2026. This chapter offers one pivotal moment from that larger journey. * ---

What This Story Taught Me
Mariatu Esther Kabba, Editor

When I chose to include my own story in this anthology, I hesitated. This book was meant to amplify other women's voices, not center my own. But as I sat with these six stories, reading them, editing them, witnessing the courage it took for each woman to share her truth I realized something: My story belongs here not because I'm the editor, but because I, too, had to choose. That night on the church floor taught me that rising isn't about comfort or safety. It's about the moment when staying small becomes more unbearable than the risk of standing tall. It's about choosing yourself even when the cost is everything you have.

Elira taught me this too, though her choice looked different from mine.

PART TWO

REBUILDING IDENTITY

Introduction

Speaking up is only the beginning.

After the moment of defiance comes the harder work: rebuilding yourself when the old structures have crumbled. What happens when you break free from oppression only to discover you've lost yourself in the process? What do you do when your identity has been so tied to survival that you no longer know who you are when you're safe?

The three women in this section faced different forms of collapse. One watched her country transform from dictatorship to democracy and had to learn what freedom actually meant. Another worked herself to the edge of death, achieving everything she thought she wanted, only to realize she'd lost herself entirely. A third woke up to explosions that shattered not just her city, but her understanding of reality itself.

These stories are about the women who had to become strangers to themselves before they could become whole. They remind us that transformation is rarely a single moment—it's a thousand small choices to keep walking forward when you no longer recognize the path.

Sometimes rising means standing up. Sometimes it means learning to stand still long enough to figure out who you're becoming.

Finding Freedom Through Truth

By Elira Canga, Journalist and communication professional, media trainer and educator, Albania

I was ten years old when communism fell in Albania.

I remember the images of the Berlin Wall coming down, the end of the dictatorship that had shaped every aspect of life in Eastern Europe for nearly half a century. At that age, I didn't know what my own dreams were yet. But I sensed the dreams my parents carried—dreams of hope, of change, of a future that nobody knew but that might finally belong to us.

My country had lived under one of Europe's most brutal communist regimes for forty-five years. We had been isolated, controlled, told what to think and how to live. And then, suddenly, it was over.

No one quite knew what freedom meant. What to do with it. How to behave in it.

Albania was moving from a long dictatorship into an unfamiliar democracy, and my generation was caught in the middle—trying to find our place in a new world while our country rebuilt itself from the ruins of isolation.

Growing up in that chaos shaped me deeply. It shaped all of us. Amid economic hardship and social upheaval, I began to dream about what my generation could contribute.

My parents were supportive but cautious. They pushed me to be a better person: dreaming big seemed risky. They feared the unknown that came with this new liberty. Nobody had lived through freedom before; we could barely recognize it. It was as if we were all learning to walk again, together, in the dark.

It became clear to me that what Albania needed most was truth—honest voices who could help people make sense of the confusion.

For the first time in decades, independent media were emerging, giving journalists the power to tell the truth freely. I knew then that this was what I wanted to do. I wanted to be part of that historic moment, to put my signature on Albania's transformation.

My family was worried. Journalism was not safe or predictable. It was uncertain, risky, full of danger.

But I couldn't ignore the pull I felt.

For the first time, people could write what they believed. They could tell their stories openly.

And I wanted to be part of that. So I chose journalism—and with it, the adventure of walking into the unknown.

Entering the Unknown

I was young, idealistic, and full of conviction that this was my mission—to tell the truth, to give voice to the people, to help make sense of this new world we were living in.

Entering journalism felt like joining a historic experiment. The profession was just being reborn in Albania—there were no roadmaps, no precedents. We were learning as we went, navigating the unknown every single day.

Those early years—the uncertainty, the chaos, the courage to dream—shaped not only my generation but who I became. We learned the meaning of freedom not from books or speeches, but by living it, by testing its boundaries, and by using our voices to build something new.

We learned that freedom is not something given—it's something you have to protect, nurture, and practice every single day.

As I grew in my career, I found myself drawn to the hardest but most meaningful stories: international and regional affairs. I reported on the war in Kosovo, the armed conflict in Macedonia, and other moments of violence and upheaval across the Balkans.

I witnessed firsthand the fragility of peace, the pain of people torn by violence, and the quiet strength of those who simply wanted to live in safety.

Those experiences changed me profoundly.

Reporting on war taught me that human suffering knows no sides. No matter which uniform people wore, their grief was the same. A mother mourning her son doesn't care about politics. A child fleeing bombs doesn't understand borders.

It taught me the importance of compassion in journalism—that beyond facts and politics, there are human stories that need to be told truthfully and with dignity.

For me, journalism was never just a profession. It was—and remains—a way of honoring that hard-won freedom, of ensuring that truth, no matter how fragile, continues to be told.

Because truth, after all, is the foundation of every free society.

And telling it—that is our shared responsibility.

The Career I Built—And the Battle I Didn't Expect

The beginning of my career felt like a dream come true. I had landed the job I always wanted, and I was deeply connected to my work. It gave me a sense of purpose and fulfillment that I deeply cherished.

But I also wanted to be a mother. That dream was just as important to me.

When my children came into my life, that was the deepest happiness I had ever known. I managed to balance my work and motherhood when they were babies and toddlers. It wasn't easy, but it was possible.

My challenge came when I was a mother of two and expecting my third child.

By that time, I had moved from journalism into media development, and I was about to take on a major new role—leading a large-scale project to transform the public broadcaster and modernize the school of journalism in Albania. It was something I had worked on tirelessly for months. The funding had finally come through. Everything was ready. And then came the moment of hesitation—not mine, but theirs.

The fact that I was a mother with two small children and another on the way suddenly became a point of concern. Managers began to doubt my ability to stay committed, to maintain focus, to deliver quality work.

It was disheartening to realize that what should have been a moment of professional triumph was now clouded by skepticism—simply because I was a woman and a mother.

If I had been a man, I believe things would have gone differently. A man in my position, who had invested months of effort, energy, and vision into the project, would have been handed the role without question.

But as a woman, I was met with doubts:

Would she take too many days off?

Would she be distracted?

Would maternity leave interfere?

Would she still have the energy?

Eventually, the project responsibilities were divided—almost as a way of saying, "You can't do it all."

But that wasn't what I had worked for. And it wasn't what I believed in.

I don't think one part of life—family or work—should be treated as a barrier to the other. I wanted both, and I believed I could have both.

I loved my job deeply, but I loved my family and my children just as much. I wanted to show them that when you truly love something, you should go after it.

What Women Carry

For women, this balance is never easy.

At the start of our careers, we may all be on equal footing. But as families grow and responsibilities multiply, the road becomes more complicated for women in ways it simply doesn't for men.

That's why we need to remind ourselves—and each other—that it can be done.

Priorities may shift with time, but that should never be an excuse to step back from your ambitions, to say no to your dream job, or to give up on a project you've poured your heart into.

There were hard days, of course.

Moments when I missed my children's activities in first grade because of a meeting I couldn't skip. Sitting in a hospital with one of my sick children, knowing I had to rush out for an important work commitment.

Those were difficult moments. But they were part of the journey.

Looking back, I see that all of it—the work, the family, the choices, the sacrifices—shaped who I am.

I've never agreed with the idea that you "can't have it all."

I believe you can have whatever you truly want—if you dedicate your time, passion, and courage to it.

There will be times when you feel weak, unmotivated, or torn between paths. But that's life—messy, demanding, and beautiful.

And it's all worth it.

The Freedom We Practice

I began this story talking about freedom—the freedom Albania gained when communism fell, the freedom I found in journalism, the freedom to tell the truth.

But I learned another kind of freedom along the way:

The freedom to define my own life. To refuse the choice between career and motherhood. To insist that I could be excellent at both.

That freedom, like the freedom my country fought for, had to be practiced every single day. It wasn't given to me. I had to claim it, protect it, and sometimes fight for it.

And I'm still fighting.

Not because it's easy, but because I want my children—especially my daughters—to grow up in a world where they never have to choose between their dreams and their families.

Where their worth isn't measured by how much they sacrifice, but by how fully they live.

That is the world I'm helping to build.

One truthful story at a time.

One courageous choice at a time.

One day at a time.

Transition

Elira learned that freedom is not something given—it must be practiced every day. But what happens when you practice so hard, push so relentlessly, that you lose sight of why you wanted freedom in the first place? Marianna's story takes us from the heights of career success to the depths of burnout and illness, and finally to a question that many of us fear to ask: What if I need to start over?

What This Story Taught Me

Mariatu Esther Kabba, Editor

Elira's story challenges one of the most persistent lies told to women: that we must choose. Choose between being a mother and being a leader. Choose between family and career. Choose between nurturing and achieving. Choose between being soft and being strong.

Elira refused to choose. And in her refusal, she exposed the lie: The "choice" was never real. It was a trap designed to keep women managing impossible trade-offs while men moved freely through the world, unencumbered by such false binaries.

What moves me most about Elira's story is her insistence on rewriting the terms. When the newsroom told her she couldn't be both a mother and a serious journalist, she didn't accept their framework. She didn't try to prove she could be "just as good as the men" by abandoning her children. She didn't shrink her ambitions to fit their expectations.

She said: "Watch me do both." And she did.

This is what revolution looks like, not in grand pronouncements, but in quiet refusals. In women who look at systems designed to limit them and say, "No. I will not accept your terms. I will create my own."

Elira's daughter grew up watching her mother lead with authority and love with tenderness. She learned that these things are not opposites. They are partners.

The woman you'll meet next—Olga—also refused to accept the terms she was given. When war came to her country, she had to decide: Will I let this define my life, or will I define my life in spite of it?

Finding Myself in a Changed World

By Olga Usenko, legal media manager, Ukraine

At 3:40 in the morning on February 24, 2022, my world split in two. I woke to an explosion. Orange light filled my window. Then another blast. And another.

I grabbed my phone. Telegram channels were flooding with reports: explosions across the entire country, missiles flying toward our cities. Every television channel showed the same thing—Putin's hour-long speech, an hour of venom directed at Ukraine, announcing what he called a "special military operation."

By 5 a.m., the air-raid sirens began. A sound that still lives in my head.

What do I do? Where do I go? My mind was chaos. I couldn't accept that this was real. I called my parents, who lived just two metro stops away. My mother's voice sounded calm: "We are fine." But their building had no shelter, and they refused to go to the metro. My own building had no shelter either, just a basement level where people stored belongings. I ran to the supermarket. People were stripping the shelves bare. No one wore masks anymore—COVID disappeared in a single morning.

The question pounded in my head: What was I supposed to do? Stay? Run? Where? How do you leave your parents behind? How do you pack your life into a single emergency backpack?

Two weeks earlier, I had been skiing in the Carpathians. I'd caught COVID on that trip—a mild case, but what followed was strange. A fog I couldn't shake. A numbing loss of focus. A sense of disconnection from myself.

My work required deep concentration: sensitive analytics, confidential interviews, delicate research with high-stakes details. Suddenly, all of it became almost impossible.

On February 23rd, the day before the invasion, I was attending a criminal law forum from home. By midday, exhaustion returned like a wave. The news had been full of rumors about a Russian invasion on February 16th, but almost no one took them seriously. My close friend in Washington, D.C. had called me multiple times, urging me to leave Ukraine "just for a week" until the hysteria passed.

I told her she was overreacting. We had lived with Russian troops near our borders before. Surely it was just another show of muscle.

That evening I went for a walk in the park with a friend to clear my mind. The city felt calm, almost disarmingly so. Then came 3:40 a.m. And everything I thought I knew shattered. When the World Changed Overnight. The first days were a blur of disbelief and frantic action.

News from Russia brought another kind of heartbreak. People I once respected—lawyers I had worked with, educated professionals, some even trained in the West—fell silent. Only two reached out with compassion, condemning their government's actions. One of them always emphasized his Ukrainian roots.

I remember asking him, "Why aren't you doing anything?"

His answer was the first time I truly felt the coldness of their mentality, the deflection, the passive acceptance: "It's Putin. The regime. We aren't responsible."

It chilled my blood.

What was even more painful was watching some friends and colleagues—especially those who had spoken the loudest about their love for Ukraine—slip away quietly before the invasion even began.

Meanwhile, the quiet ones, those who never asked to be seen as heroes, stepped forward with calm resolve and went to defend the country. Their example changed my understanding of strength and reminded me that true patriotism never needs an audience.

From the first day of the invasion, all of us began sending money to the Ukrainian Armed Forces, fundraising for helmets, drones, medical kits, Starlinks. Supporting friends, colleagues, and relatives at the front. Checking in with those who had survived occupation.

We rediscovered our culture—the songs, the language, the traditions—not as symbols, but as shields against annihilation. And we let go of Russian culture entirely. For good.

As months passed, I lost relatives in Moscow—not to death, but to propaganda. They repeated the same narratives: "Ukraine bombed Donbas for eight years..." Even though none of them had ever set foot there.

I realized that some relationships do not survive truth. Maybe they are not meant to.

Just Live Your Life

The truth is, the transformation didn't happen in one moment. It unfolded hour by hour, day by day, as the country learned to breathe under sirens and constant power outages.

Like millions of Ukrainians, I found myself choosing every day to live, to show up, to help, to dream. The fear didn't disappear, but it stopped paralyzing me.

There is a saying in Ukraine that captures our transformation: "just live your life." To me, it means live here and now, despite everything.

Walking through Kyiv during the day, you see life everywhere—cafés are full, theaters sold out months ahead, a vibrant hunger to live in the present. And yet, the moment the sirens sound, something shifts inside your chest—a tightening, a familiar wave of anxiety.

What surprised me most was this: under extreme stress, something inside me strengthened. I began to value every day in a way I never had before. When physical danger becomes part of daily life, you start to see the world differently. Gratitude becomes a survival mechanism. Everything and everyone unnecessary falls away.

Businesses found ways to survive, including the legal publishing house I worked for. We shrank, went fully online, lost talented people—a huge challenge for any media. Yet our clients supported us. We supported them. The war reshaped our business life into something unprecedented: mutual aid, trust, solidarity.

Eventually, life led me to the United States. I often say that the universe has its own plans for us. A year earlier, I had a completely different vision of my future. Now I no longer plan too far ahead. I see my purpose differently: to bring the Ukrainian perspective into every room I enter.

What the War Taught Me

Living through war taught me resilience I didn't know existed. What surprised me most is that we Ukrainians can experience extreme stress and still somehow preserve our optimism. It's almost paradoxical. But it is now a core part of our national character.

Our collective identity shifted from disappointment and exhaustion to a deep understanding of who we are. The war reshaped our social relationships. I have never seen Ukrainians care for one another the way we do now. Mutual aid has become instinctive. Interpersonal trust has grown in ways that would have seemed impossible before.

I changed too.

I learned that I can endure more than I ever imagined.

I learned to let go of illusions—especially about people who chose comfort over truth.

I learned that courage is often quiet. Those colleagues on the frontline don't show up on social media in bulletproof vests. They simply do what needs to be done.

I learned to find purpose in chaos, and meaning in small things: a quiet morning without sirens, a coffee with my favorite oat milk, a message from a friend, a normal day that feels like a gift.

I now understand that survival is not the same as living. And living is not the same as thriving. Yet somehow, in the darkest years of our history, Ukrainians learned to do all three at once.

A Message for Anyone in the Dark

If you are going through your own hard moment right now—whether it's war, illness, loss, or simply the weight of uncertainty—I want you to know this:

You don't have to feel brave to act bravely.

Your strength might appear quietly, in the smallest decisions—getting out of bed, taking a walk, calling someone you trust. Transformation rarely feels like transformation when you're in it. It feels like surviving.

And remember: you never rise alone.

There is always someone ready to stand with you—sometimes a friend, sometimes a stranger, sometimes an entire nation.

The fog I felt in those early weeks after COVID wasn't just physical. It was my mind and body trying to process what was about to come. But when the explosions came, the fog lifted. Clarity arrived not in comfort, but in crisis.

I learned that we are capable of more than we imagine. That normal days are sacred. That community is not a luxury—it is survival. And I learned that choosing to live fully, even when the sirens are sounding, is the most powerful form of resistance.

So whatever your war is—whatever is trying to break you—remember: You are stronger than you think. You are not alone. And you can choose, every single day, to keep living your life.

What This Story Taught Me

Mariatu Esther Kabba, Editor

Olga's story asks a question I'm not sure I could answer: How do you choose life when death is all around you?

When missiles fly at 3:40 a.m. When your country is at war. When everything you knew is gone. When friends become enemies over propaganda. When the future is uncertain and the present is unbearable.

How do you choose to keep living fully?

Olga's answer: You decide that the war doesn't get to take everything.

It can take safety. It can take certainty. It can take peace. But it cannot take your humanity, your capacity for joy, your right to love and create and hope—unless you give it permission.

And Olga refused.

What strikes me most about her story is not the dramatic moments—though those are there, vivid and terrifying. What strikes me is the ordinary defiance. The decision to celebrate a birthday during war. The choice to maintain friendships even when it's complicated. The insistence on beauty and culture and meaning when survival alone would have been enough.

This is a particular kind of courage: not the courage to fight, but the courage to live.

Olga reminds us that resistance isn't always loud. Sometimes it's quiet. Sometimes it's simply refusing to let crisis steal your joy, your relationships, your sense of self.

Sometimes rising means choosing to bloom even in rubble.

The next woman—Marianna—also learned that sometimes the bravest thing you can do is start over when everything falls apart.

I Chose to Rise

By Marianna Brandão de Arimathéia e Silva, Business development leader and storyteller, Brazil

I grew up in a very feminine world.

My childhood was filled with women: grandmothers, my mother, aunts, and cousins. Many of them were teachers, women of faith, active in their churches and communities. They were strong in quiet ways—they worked, cared for others, organized the house, and supported the family. They didn't use words like "empowerment" or "leadership," but that is what they practiced every single day.

Around the table, with coffee, food, and conversation, I learned my first lessons about life. I watched them solve problems, support each other, and face difficulties with dignity. They taught me values not through speeches but through example: responsibility, faith, generosity, and resilience.

In this environment, a very curious girl was born.

As a child, I loved stories, music, nature, and watching people. Books and songs were my first ways of traveling beyond my neighborhood. My father, a man ahead of his time who was deeply passionate about music, art, and sports, shaped my love for culture and the wider world. Early on, like him, I sensed that life was much larger than what I could see and that one day, I would venture out to meet it.

When it was time to choose a career, this curiosity turned into direction. I studied International Relations because I wanted to understand how countries, cultures, and people connect. My biggest dream was to become a diplomat—represent Brazil, live abroad, take part in international decisions. It seemed like the perfect combination of purpose and adventure. But real life and dreams sometimes move on different timelines.

Finding My Path in Business

A diplomatic career in Brazil is highly competitive and, in many ways, elitist. It demands years of preparation, time, and money—resources I didn't have. I needed to work early to help at home, pay for university, and build my independence. There was no way to stop everything and dedicate my life to one exam.

So instead of the theoretical world of diplomacy, I was pushed into the practical world of business.

To my surprise, I liked it.

I joined companies working with technology, innovation, and new ideas. Little by little, I moved closer to international business—foreign clients, trade fairs, negotiations in other languages. I discovered that my dream of a global life could exist in the private sector too, by connecting companies from different countries and opening new markets.

Over time, I grew into management roles. I learned how to lead teams, close deals, and navigate complex negotiations. I spent many years working with LED display technology and became known in a very specific market niche. My name started to be associated with results, problem-solving, and making things happen even in difficult situations.

The market likes this profile. And for a while, I did too.

The Cost of Carrying Everything

I began to repeat the image of the "super woman"—the one who can handle everything, works long hours, travels constantly, responds to messages at any hour, and never says no.

I was proud to be that person. The one who carried a lot, delivered under pressure, and never broke.

What I didn't see was that, slowly, I was disappearing inside that role.

Burnout didn't arrive in one day. It appeared in small signs: sleepless nights, constant irritation, lack of patience, difficulty enjoying even good moments. I couldn't relax. I didn't know how to "do nothing" without feeling guilty. My whole identity was tied to work.

I was what I produced.

Then came the first big professional fall—changes in the company, decisions outside my control, projects that ended. On the surface, it was just part of the business world. Inside, it felt like a collapse.

Without that position and that level of activity, who was I?

It was a painful question, but an important one.

I started waking up with my heart racing, asking myself, "How did I get here?" The Brazilian writer Guimarães Rosa wrote that life heats and cools, tightens and loosens, calms and then uncalms, and that what it wants from us is courage.

I felt that my life was in that uncalm phase.

Everything inside me was asking for change.

Choosing to Start Again

A simple but deep question began to grow in my heart: Was I going to keep living to protect an image, or would I have the courage to start again?

At forty, I chose to start again.

That meant admitting that I wanted a different kind of life. I wanted to study again, live abroad, have more balance, experience a more mature love, and work with more purpose and less automatic pressure.

This choice didn't arrive as a heroic moment. It was a process of conversations, silence, tears, and many prayers.

My relationship with God has always been very personal. I talk to Him simply about my fears, my gratitude, and my confusion. During that period, my prayer was often, "Show me the way. I am afraid, but I am willing to go."

Slowly, doors began to open. The idea of doing a master's degree abroad, which had been a distant dream, started to become a real possibility.

I was arranging my life for this big shift when another piece of news changed everything again:

A breast cancer diagnosis.

When Everything Became Clear

I remember the doctor's office, the serious look, the feeling that time had slowed around me. When the word "cancer" is spoken to you, everything becomes very real and very fast.

All my plans—the master's program, the move to another country, the new stage of my career—were not cancelled, but they were clearly placed on hold. There was now one main priority: my health.

People often ask if I felt afraid. Of course there were moments of fear—fear of the unknown, of treatment, of how my body would change. But I also felt something that surprised me: a quiet kind of courage. Not dramatic, not for anyone to see. Just a firm inner decision to face what needed to be faced, one step at a time.

The six months of treatment were intense. My body became slower, more tired, more sensitive. I had to respect limits I had ignored before.

Yet as my body became more fragile, something inside me became more awake.

I started to notice small things: someone bringing soup, a message arriving at the right moment, a visit, a prayer said for me. Once again, the women in my family carried me. My sister stayed strong when I no longer had enough strength. The love of my mother and my niece became the fuel that kept me going.

I realized that I didn't need to be strong all the time. I was allowed to receive care. I was allowed to rest.

During this time, the phrase "she chose to rise" gained new meaning. Rising wasn't about winning a battle in a glamorous way. It meant getting out of bed on a hard day. Going to one more treatment session. Allowing myself to cry without staying trapped in despair.

I didn't choose cancer, but I could choose how I would walk through that valley.

I also had to rebuild my relationship with my own body. The scars, the changes, the fatigue—all of this became part of my story. At first, there was strangeness when I looked in the mirror. Later, there was a kind of respect.

My body was not my enemy. It was doing its best to keep me alive.

After six months, I finally heard the words I most wanted to hear: the treatment had worked. I was in remission. I was considered cured.

The doctor told me calmly that it was time to return to my life, my plans, and my dreams.

But "go back to normal" had a different weight for me. I didn't want to go back to my old normal, because my old normal was not healthy.

I wanted a new way of living.

A New Chapter in Arizona

From that point on, every decision carried an internal question: Does this honor the life I almost lost and then received again?

With that awareness, I returned to the plan that had been waiting for me: a master's degree in Global Management at Thunderbird in Arizona.

Arriving on campus was emotional. The strong sun, the dry air, the mix of accents, the flags from so many countries, the energy of people from all over the world with their own dreams—it all reminded me that the world really was larger than the life I had lived before.

I was no longer the LED market expert or the "super manager." I was simply a student again. In my forties, with many years of experience and a recent medical history, I was starting over with a notebook in my hand and an open heart.

Studying in English required another layer of courage. My vocabulary wasn't perfect, my accent showed where I came from, and I had to work harder in some classes. But after everything I'd been through, this was just one more challenge, not a wall.

I decided that I didn't need to be the best in the room. I needed to be honest with my process.

Instead of judging myself for every mistake, I began to celebrate small victories: a presentation that went well, a paper I was proud of, a conversation where I felt more fluent. Little by little, the girl who loved the world from far away, the professional who lost herself in work, and the woman who faced cancer began to come together into a more whole version of myself.

In the middle of all these changes, love also found its place. I met a partner with whom I could be fully myself—with my past, my scars, my hopes, and my faith. It wasn't a story of someone who arrived to save me. Some people come to walk beside us, to share the weight, to laugh, to plan, and to support.

After an experience like cancer, you look at relationships differently. You value presence, honesty, and kindness more than perfection.

What I Learned About Rising

The biggest transformation after the cure was not only in my body or my career. It was in my identity.

I stopped defining myself by my job title, my productivity, or my ability to hold everything together. I started asking myself different questions:

Am I living according to my values?

Am I taking care of my body and my mind?

Am I present with the people I love?

Does my work contribute to something beyond my ego?

For me, "She Chose to Rise" is not just a beautiful phrase. It describes a choice I have made many times.

I chose to rise when I faced burnout and admitted that I needed a different path.

I chose to rise when I heard the word "cancer" and decided to walk through treatment with as much calm and faith as I could.

I chose to rise when I moved to another country, sat in a classroom again, and spoke in a language that was not my own.

I keep choosing to rise every time I remember that my story is still being written.

If I could speak directly to a woman who is tired, sick, confused, or starting over later than she expected, I would tell her this:

You do not need to be a heroine. You do not need a perfect plan. You only need the next honest step.

Sometimes rising is something small and very practical: booking a medical exam, asking for help, applying for a course, sending a CV, leaving a situation that hurts you, or starting a ten-minute walk each day.

It is not always about big gestures. Often it is about consistency, honesty, and a little bit of faith.

I am not a perfect success story. I am a work in progress. I am healed and still attentive. I am strong and still sensitive. I am global and at the same time deeply rooted in my origins.

My roots are non-negotiable. I carry Brazil with me—its warmth, resilience, and joy, and the values my family taught me about dignity, hard work, and care for others. I can adapt to new cultures, but adaptation is not imitation. I grow outward without losing my center.

If there is one message I hope my story can leave, it is this:

Life will change our plans. Sometimes gently, sometimes in very hard ways. Even then, we still have the power to choose. To stand up again. To adjust the route. To keep walking.

That, for me, is what it means to say: She chose to rise.

Transition

Marianna chose to rebuild her life on her own terms—at forty, in a new country, as a student again. But sometimes, we don't get to choose when transformation comes. Sometimes it arrives at 3:40 in the morning with the sound of explosions. Olga's story reminds us that even when the world around us is falling apart, we still have the power to decide who we will become in the rubble

What This Story Taught Me

Mariatu Esther Kabba, Editor

Marianna's story is a reminder that rising isn't a one-time event.

She rose when she built a successful career. She fell when burnout consumed her. She rose when she left that career to find herself. She fell when cancer came. She rose when she chose treatment and fought. She fell when grief and fear overwhelmed her. She rose again.

And again. And again.

This is what we need to normalize: Rising is not linear. It's cyclical. It's seasonal. Some days you're soaring. Some days you're crawling. Both are part of the same journey.

What moved me most about Marianna's story is her willingness to start over at forty. In a culture that tells women our value diminishes with age, that our best years are behind us, that reinvention is for the young—Marianna said, "No. I'm not done becoming."

She walked away from the career she'd built. She faced her health crisis. She rebuilt her life on different terms, terms that prioritized meaning over achievement, presence over productivity, being over doing.

And in doing so, she became more herself than she'd ever been. This is the gift Marianna offers us: permission to begin again. Permission to shed what no longer fits. Permission to say, "That version of success doesn't work for me anymore. I'm creating a new one."

The final woman in this section—Dr. Adelaida—will show us what it means to keep rising even after the deepest loss.

PART THREE

LIVING IN YOUR POWER

Introduction

There's a moment in every woman's journey when she stops asking permission. She stops waiting to be chosen. Stops apologizing for taking up space. Stops shrinking herself to fit into rooms that were never built for her in the first place.

This is the moment she begins to live in her power.

Dr. Adelaida Severson's story closes this collection because it embodies what all the women before her have been moving toward: a life lived on her own terms, defined by her own measures of success. She has been underestimated, overlooked, and told she didn't belong. She has built businesses, raised sons, buried the love of her life. She has failed spectacularly and risen beautifully.

And through it all, she has learned that power isn't about dominance or perfection. It's about faith, family, failure, philanthropy, and the quiet strength of femininity.

Her story—and the framework she offers—is both a testament to her journey and a roadmap for ours.

Because in the end, rising is not a destination. It's a practice. A daily choice to show up for ourselves, for our communities, for the women who will come after us.

These seven women—from Sierra Leone to Ukraine, from Bangladesh to Brazil—have shown us what's possible when we refuse to stay down.

Now it's our turn.

Finding Success in the "F" Word

By Adelaida V. Severson, Ph.D., President and CEO of Bushtex, Inc., USA

"Are you here to take the notes for the meeting?"

The three-star General didn't look up as he asked. Around the table, a dozen men in uniform settled into their seats. I was the only woman in the room. The only civilian.

"No," I said, keeping my voice steady. "I'm Dr. Adelaida Severson, and I'm here as the Subject Matter Expert to explain how the satellite coverage will work."

The silence that followed was brief but loaded. Then we began.

This wasn't the first time I'd been underestimated, and it wouldn't be the last. Years earlier, a news director had looked me in the eye and said, "You don't have the look we need for the anchor position. Blonde and blue-eyed is what keeps our ratings up." Later, a doctor would deliver different words with the same finality: "There's nothing more we can do for your husband."

Each of these moments broke something in me. And each time, I chose to rise from the breaking.

I was born in Pearl City, Hawaii, not far from Pearl Harbor, the youngest of three children in a modest household. My father was fifty when I was born, my mother forty—unusual for the 1960s. I didn't realize how old they were until sixth grade, when my father came to a school event where I was the emcee. My teacher smiled and said, "How wonderful that your grandfather could come!"

That was the first time I understood I was different.

My father owned a well-known bar in Waikiki. On Saturday mornings, he'd take me to the market, navigating the stalls with confidence, negotiating with vendors, picking the best vegetables and fish. He'd introduce me proudly: "This is my daughter." Not granddaughter. Daughter.

His friends became my mentors—teaching me how to speak well, how to carry myself, how to read people. On my sixteenth birthday, my father took me on a date to show me how a man should treat a woman: opening doors, dressing well, showing respect. Those lessons stayed with me.

Most of my career mentors would also be men—not by choice, but by necessity. In the fields I entered, there simply weren't many women in leadership. And the few who were there often felt they had to guard their positions rather than lift others up.

My mother had a different kind of strength. Born and raised in the Philippines, she earned her master's degree at the conservatory there and was later accepted into a broadcasting school in Washington, D.C.—the only woman in a class of twenty white men.

She became a radio announcer in Hawaii, the voice of home for Filipino migrant workers in the pineapple and sugar cane fields. She spoke their language, sang their folk songs, brought them news from the world they'd left behind. When my siblings and I were born, she became a homemaker. But by the time I was a toddler, she returned to broadcasting.

I have vivid memories of her working from our dining room—playing piano, singing, reading the news between songs, shushing me when the red light came on to signal she was live on air. She was, in many ways, the first podcaster—decades ahead of her time.

I wanted to be just like her.

In high school, I was the classic overachiever: class president, band member, oboist in orchestra, flag girl in marching band. When it came time to look at colleges, my guidance counselor told me something I'd never heard before.

"You're a three-fer," he said. "Female, minority, and poor. Colleges on the mainland will want you. You'll get scholarships."

I didn't know what "minority" meant. In Hawaii, we were a true melting pot—Hawaiian, Portuguese, Filipino, Japanese, Chinese. We all had our stereotypes, sure. Hawaiians were lazy. Portuguese weren't the smartest. Filipinos wore bright clothes and ate strange food. Japanese were cliquish. Chinese were frugal. But it wasn't racist—it was just who we were. We laughed about it together.

To be called a minority was news to me.

I went to the University of Southern California on a near-full scholarship. My parents still couldn't afford it, so Pell Grants, work study, and small loans carried me through four years. I double-majored in Broadcast Journalism and International Relations, dreaming of becoming a foreign correspondent. Life, as it turns out, had other plans.

The Breaking Point

I was hired right out of college as a television reporter. Back then, you did everything yourself—reporting, writing, editing, camera work. In journalism school, they'd drilled into us: be tough, be accurate, be first. No room for error.

But television was also a business. Your looks mattered more than your skills because it was all about ratings, and ratings sold advertising. I learned this quickly as I tried to work my way up.

I wanted to be on camera, a main reporter, maybe an anchor. But I kept hearing the same message, delivered in different ways: "You don't have the look we want. Blonde and blue-eyed is what sells."

I kept pushing anyway. Kept believing that one day, things would change.

Then came the fire.

I was first on the scene that morning, the building already engulfed, flames shooting into the sky. Perfect B-roll. Great television. As I stood there writing my script for the live shot, preparing to deliver my report at the top of the hour, a thought cut through everything else:

People are dying in that building.

And all I care about is my story.

The realization hit me like cold water. Was this the life I wanted? Was I going to keep fighting an uphill battle in an industry that didn't want me—while chasing stories about other people's tragedies just to prove I belonged?

I was at a crossroads.

Then, as if the universe had been listening, a college friend called. He'd started a satellite communications company and needed someone with broadcasting and international experience to run his international broadcasts.

I didn't even know what satellite communications was.

But I took the leap anyway.

Love and Risk

The satellite communications world was a whirlwind. We did live Pay-Per-View events in Vegas—championship fights, concerts, HBO comedy specials with Whoopi Goldberg. It was the late eighties, early nineties. Everything was new, fast, high-stakes.

And that's where I met Barry.

He was based in Phoenix, covering Phoenix Suns games and Pac-10 sports while I worked out of our Los Angeles headquarters. We fell in love across state lines, connected by satellites and shared ambition.

Eventually, we decided to break away and start our own company. I left a secure job in LA and moved to Phoenix—another leap of faith. We weren't even married yet.

Our first major contract came from CBS News: cover the first Gulf War in 1991. Barry would be sent to Jordan, then into Iraq, to provide live satellite coverage of the conflict.

I moved back to Hawaii to care for my aging parents. In our culture, putting your parents in assisted living was unthinkable. So I cared for them while working part-time in local television news.

Then the call came.

Barry had been kidnapped on the border between Iran and Iraq. Missing, along with two other journalists.

I remember watching the news in Hawaii and seeing his face on the screen—his photo next to the other two men. This was the time when militants would put black hoods over hostages' heads and behead them on camera.

He was missing for two weeks.

I prayed in ways I had never prayed before. Bargaining with God. Begging. Promising anything if Barry could just come home alive.

Somehow—miraculously—they were found. He was released.

And we made a promise to each other: we would build something together. A life. A family. A business that mattered.

Building and Breaking

Building a business from scratch is hard. Building it with your spouse is harder. But Barry and I learned to stay in our lanes, to respect boundaries, to support without smothering.

It wasn't easy. Cash flow was inconsistent. Barry traveled constantly to dangerous regions. Insurance companies wouldn't cover us—too high-risk, they said. Clients paid late or not at all.

I went back to school, earning my master's degree at Arizona State University. I took a job there as Director of Special Events for the University President so we could get the health benefits our business desperately needed. I loved the work so much that I kept going—eventually pursuing my Ph.D.

Then life got complicated.

The university president retired. I was ABD—all but dissertation. I had a three-year-old son at home. And I was pregnant with twins.

It was time to make a choice: keep working for someone else, or build our business and raise our family.

I chose us.

Let me tell you—writing a dissertation while pregnant with twins, caring for a toddler, and keeping clients happy does not make for a pleasant version of Adelaida. I was exhausted. Overwhelmed. Cranky as hell. But I finished. We built the business. We raised three sons—Lars, Brock, and Swen—all of whom graduated from college and found their own paths. Barry and I were married for thirty-three years.

Until April 2024, when I lost him to lung cancer.

The Five F-Words

People ask me all the time: "How do you do it? Run a company, serve on boards, mentor others, grieve your husband, and still show up for your life?"

The answer sounds crude, but it's honest: it's the F-word.

Not the one you're thinking—though I've dropped plenty of those too, especially in a male-dominated industry. No, I mean the F-words that have actually carried me through: the ones that ground me, guide me, and keep me rising when life knocks me down.

There are five that matter most.

Faith

Faith in something bigger than myself. Faith in myself. Faith in the people I love and lead.

I grew up in a Filipino Catholic household where Baby Jesus was the center of everything. We went to church constantly, prayed rosaries, lit candles. I didn't fully understand it as a child. But as I grew older, faith became the thing that grounded me when I needed control and learned I couldn't have it.

God will not give you anything He knows you cannot handle. I've tested that promise more times than I can count.

When Barry was kidnapped, I prayed like my life depended on it—because his did. When the cancer diagnosis came, I prayed again. When he died, faith was the only thing that kept me standing.

But faith isn't just about religion. It's about believing in yourself when no one else does. It's about having confidence in the people you lead—your employees, your children, your partner. If they know you believe in them, they'll move mountains.

Family

"Everyone needs a house to live in, but a supportive family is what builds a home."

Family doesn't always mean blood. It's the friend who listens without judgment. The colleague who picks up the slack when you're falling apart. The neighbor who brings you soup when you're sick.

Family practices kindness and care. Family doesn't leave each other behind or step on each other to get ahead.

My father and his friends mentored me when women wouldn't. My mother showed me what it meant to be a pioneer. Barry became my partner in every sense of the word. And now, my sons carry forward everything we built together.

Find your tribe. Create families of your own—through friendships, networks, circles of trust. These are the people who will keep you warm when the world feels cold.

Failure

Growing up in an Asian household, failure was not an option. An A-minus felt like an F. I was terrified of making mistakes, of stepping outside my comfort zone.

Now? I've failed more times than I can count. We even went through bankruptcy. And honestly, I wouldn't have it any other way.

Failure builds character. It forces you to look at what you've taken for granted. It makes you innovate, think creatively, take risks.

The fire that made me question my career in television? That was a failure—I'd lost sight of what mattered. But it pushed me toward something better.

Failure taught me that strength isn't about never falling. It's about pulling up your big-girl pants and keeping going.

Philanthropy

While this work doesn't start with an "F" phonetically it does. My mother used to say, "It is a blessing to be blessed so you can bless others. When you give, it comes back to you tenfold."

Giving back doesn't always mean money. You can give time, talent, or treasure. All three matter.

I serve on boards. I mentor young women. I show up for my community. Not because I have to, but because it gives my life purpose beyond my own success.

Whether it's buying Girl Scout cookies, volunteering your expertise, or mentoring someone who reminds you of your younger self—do it. It will make you a better person and a greater contributor to the world.

Femininity

Here's what I want every woman to know: you will never be a man. And you shouldn't want to be.

We are better, stronger, and smarter. Don't compete with men on their terms. Have standards. Have grace. Turn pressure into power. Plan like a CEO and shine like a queen.

You don't have to be the loudest person in the room. Sometimes the scariest thing alive is a quiet woman who knows her worth.

Speak with intention. Be thoughtful. Be kind—even when others aren't.

Meet hate with love. I know that sounds cliché, but in a world full of divisiveness, class and dignity will always resonate louder than anger.

Rising, Again and Again

Those are my F-words. What are yours?

You don't have to choose the letter F. But I encourage you to find the words that will carry you when life gets hard—because it will get hard. The words that remind you who you are and what you stand for.

One day, your life will flash before your eyes.

Make sure it's worth watching.

I've been underestimated, dismissed, and told I didn't belong more times than I can count. I've been assumed to be the note-taker when I was the expert. I've been rejected for not having the "right look." I've lost the love of my life.

And I'm still here.

Still rising.

Because that's what we do. We rise for ourselves. We rise for our families. We rise for the women who come after us.

So go. Be bold. Take risks. Fail spectacularly. Love deeply. Give generously.

And when life knocks you down—and it will—remember the F-words.

Then get back up.

What This Story Taught Me
Mariatu Esther Kabba, Editor

Dr. Adelaida taught me that true success is measured not by what you achieve but by what you give and who you become.

Her five F-words—Faith, Family, Failure, Philanthropy, and Femininity—aren't just a framework for success. They're a roadmap for a meaningful life.

What strikes me most about Adelaida's story is her insistence that women don't need to compete with men on men's terms. We don't need to become like them to be taken seriously. We don't need to abandon our femininity to claim our power.

We need to redefine power entirely.

Adelaida shows us what that looks like: Building businesses with your spouse. Raising sons who respect women. Facing loss and grief and still showing up with grace. Still leading. Still giving. Still mattering.

Even after burying the love of her life. Even after thirty-three years of partnership ended. Even in grief, Adelaida continues to rise not by pretending the loss doesn't hurt, but by honoring what was while building what's next.

She reminds us that you can be powerful and tender. Ambitious and nurturing. Successful and faithful. These are not contradictions. They are completeness.

"One day, your life will flash before your eyes. Make sure it's worth watching."

Adelaide has lived a life worth watching. Not because she avoided pain or loss or failure, but because she transformed them into wisdom, generosity, and purpose.

As you move into the Afterword, I invite you to reflect: What does rising mean for you? What will make your life worth watching?

Afterword

What Happens When Women Choose to Rise

When I began this project, I asked: What if women across the world could speak to each other, across borders, languages, and cultures, and discover they are not alone?

Now, after walking alongside six women from eight countries, I have my answer.

We are not alone. We have never been alone.

The woman in Ukraine hiding in a basement while missiles fly overhead shares something profound with the woman in Sierra Leone fighting for her education after losing her father. The woman in Bangladesh navigating cultural expectations around beauty carries the same weight as the woman in the Brazilian rebuilding her identity after cancer. The American woman restructuring a system never built with her in mind, a Djibouti finding her voice and identity through arts and literature speaks the same language of becoming as the Albanian journalist proving she can be both mother and leader.

Their struggles look different. Their contexts are worlds apart. Their solutions are shaped by geography, culture, economics, and opportunity. But their essence, the moment of choosing to rise—is identical.

I thought I was creating a book. What I actually created was a mirror.

In these pages, women from every corner of the earth can see themselves reflected back. Not in the specific circumstances, most of us will never experience war, or poverty at that level, or stalking, or the particular challenges each contributor faced. But in the feeling. In the moment when everything falls apart and you have to decide: Will I let this break me, or will I use these broken pieces to build something new?

That moment is universal.

What surprised me most in this process was not the diversity of our struggles, but the similarity of our strength. I expected to find different kinds of courage. What I found instead was courage expressing itself in different languages, different contexts, different circumstances—but always, always rooted in the same source: a deep knowing that staying down is not an option. That our daughters are watching. That our grandmothers endured worse with less. We owe it to ourselves, to each other, and most importantly to God to keep rising and to fully live out our potential and purpose.

I also ddn't expect how much these women would teach me, not just through their stories, but through the process of sharing them. Elita taught me that frozen isn't the same as weak. Zineb taught me that beauty standards are just history and geography written on our bodies. Marianna taught me that sometimes the bravest thing we can do is start over at forty. Olga taught me that choosing life in the middle of death is a revolutionary act. Dr. Adelaida taught me that success without meaning is just noise. Elira taught me that you don't have to choose between being a mother and being a leader, you can rewrite the terms entirely.

And in curating their stories, I learned something about my own: that my rising is not separate from theirs. That when I amplify their voices, I find my own. That the work of gathering women's stories is not just documentation, it is ministry. It is resistance. It is love.

This book began as a whisper in my spirit. It became a conversation across continents. And now, I hope, it becomes a movement.

The Lessons

If you read these seven stories carefully, and went through my reflection on each, if you let them settle into your bones, you'll discover that they teach us at least five essential truths about what it means to rise. These truths are not sentimental. They are hard-won, tested in fire, and proven in lived experience.

Rising Is Not Linear

This may be the most important lesson in this entire book.

None of these women rose once and stayed risen. They rose, stumbled, fell, got back up, rose again, had setbacks, climbed higher, dealt with new challenges, and discovered that the rising never actually ends. It's not a destination. It's a practice.

Elita didn't lock her stalker in that music shop and suddenly became fearless forever. She still has days when anxiety grips her. Olga didn't survive the first year of war and achieve permanent peace. She lives with ongoing uncertainty, still navigating loss, still choosing courage daily. Dr. Adelaida didn't bury her husband after thirty-three years and arrived at some final state of healing. She's still becoming, still growing, still wrestling with grief and joy simultaneously.

We have been sold a lie about transformation. We've been told that healing is linear, that progress moves in one direction, that once you "overcome," you're done. But these stories reveal a different truth: Rising is cyclical. It's seasonal. Some days you're soaring. Some days you're crawling. Both are part of the same journey.

This matters because so many women give up on themselves when they have a setback. They think, "I thought I was past this. I thought I had healed. I thought I had risen." And when the old wound reopens or the old fear returns or the old pattern resurfaces, they interpret it as failure.

But what if it's not failure? What if it's just... being human?

What if rising looks like this: You climb. You rest. You slip. You catch yourself. You climb again. You reach a plateau. You stay there for a while. You find a new path. You take a different route. You help someone else climb. You realize you're higher than you were, but not where you thought you'd be. You keep going anyway.

The women in this book teach us that resilience is not about never falling. It's about always getting back up. It's about knowing that the fall doesn't erase the climb. It's about understanding that strength isn't measured by how long you stay elevated—it's measured by how many times you choose to rise again.

Rising Requires Witness

Look closely at these stories and you'll notice something: Not one of these women rose alone.

Elita had friends who believed her when others dismissed her fear. Zineb had a mother who absorbed her pain and a father who valued her mind. Marianna had colleagues and mentors who saw her worth beyond her corporate performance. Olga has a global community that refused to let her country be forgotten. Dr. Adelaida had a husband who partnered with her for thirty-three years and children who remind her daily why her voice matters. Elira had editors who gave her a chance and a daughter who inspired her to keep fighting.

And I had foster parents who gave me a family, a mother who taught me survival, mentors who invested in my potential, and organizations that bet on a girl from Freetown with big dreams.

Rising requires witness. We cannot do this alone. We were never meant to.

Someone has to see us—really see us—in our struggle and say, "I believe you. I believe in you. I'm here." Someone has to hold space for our pain without trying to fix it. Someone has to remind us who we are when we've forgotten. Someone has to refuse to let us give up on ourselves.

This is why representation matters. This is why mentorship matters. This is why community matters. This is why movements matter.

When we witness each other's rising, when we show up, speak up, hold space, and refuse to look away, we create the conditions that make transformation possible.

So, here's my question for you: Who witnessed your rising? Who held the door open, who believed you when you didn't believe yourself, who stayed when others left? Have you thanked them? Have you told them what their witness meant?

And more importantly: Who are you witnessing right now? What woman in your life is in her rubble moment, and are you showing up for her? Are you seeing her, believing her, making space for her truth?

Because here's what I know: We rise because someone witnessed us. And we witness others so they can rise too. It's a sacred chain, an unbroken line of women lifting women, stretching back through our mothers and grandmothers and great-grandmothers, and forward through our daughters and granddaughters and the women who will come after us.

Don't break the chain.

Rising Is Communal

These women didn't rise for themselves alone. They couldn't.

Elita rose so other women would know that stalking is not flattery, it's terrorism, and it deserves to be named and stopped. Zineb rose so girls everywhere would understand that their worth is not determined by other people's limited imaginations. Marianna rose so women facing illness or burnout would see that starting over is not failure, it's wisdom. Olga rose to remind the world that Ukrainian lives matter, that war is not an abstraction, that choosing life in the face of death is both ordinary and extraordinary. Dr. Adelaida rose to show that even after burying the love of your life, even after losing your partner of thirty-three years, you can still redefine success, still lead with purpose, still find meaning in giving back. Elira rose to prove that mothers don't have to shrink themselves to fit into spaces not designed for them.

And I rise daily, imperfectly, repeatedly, so that women in Sierra Leone and across Africa and around the world will see that a fatherless daughter from Freetown can amplify voices on a global stage. That poverty and loss and discrimination are not the end of the story. That our stories matter. That we matter.

When a woman rises, she doesn't rise for herself alone. She rises for her daughter who is watching. She rises for her mother who couldn't. She rises for her sister who is still in her rubble moment. She rises for the women who will come after her and need to know it's possible.

This is what Maya Angelou meant when she said, "Each time a woman stands up for herself, she stands up for all women."

Our rising is communal. It always has been.

Think about the suffragettes who fought for our right to vote. They rose for us. Think about the women who demanded equal pay, who fought for reproductive rights, who challenged laws that treated us as property, they rose for us. Think about the women who broke barriers in medicine, law, politics, business, media, and every field that tried to keep them out—they rose for us.

We stand on their shoulders. And now, women are standing on ours.

This means our rising is not optional. It's not just about our personal healing or our individual success. When we rise, we create proof that rising is possible. We create pathways for the women who will follow. We shift the entire landscape.

So, when you're tempted to stay small, remember: You're not just rising for yourself. You're rising for every woman who needs to see that it can be done. You're rising for your daughter. You're rising for the girl in your community who is watching you, wondering if she matters, wondering if her voice counts, wondering if she, too, can rise.

Your rising lifts us all.

Rising Is Contextual

Here is where we must be honest about complexity.

What it means to rise in Ukraine—a country under invasion, where survival is the daily victory is different from what it means to rise in the United States, where the battles are often systemic but not actively life-threatening in the same way. What it means to rise in Sierra Leone, where resources are scarce and systems are fragile, is different from what it means to rise in Albania, where democracy is young but infrastructure is more stable.

We cannot flatten these differences in the name of universality. We cannot pretend that all women face the same barriers or have access to the same resources or carry the same risks when they speak up.

Olga's rising looks like continuing to live, work, and create while missiles fly. My rising looked like sleeping on a church floor because I chose my voice over shelter. Elita's rising looked like locking a predator in a room and calling the police, a privilege many women globally do not have because their police forces don't take violence against women seriously. Marianna's rising included access to healthcare that saved her life from cancer, healthcare that millions of women will never receive.

Context matters. Geography matters. Economics matter. Race matters. Citizenship matters. Access matters.

When we talk about rising, we must acknowledge that some women are rising from rubble, while others are rising from inconvenience. Some women are fighting for survival, while others are fighting for success. Some women risk their lives by speaking, while others risk their comfort.

All of it matters. None of it is less valid. But we must name the differences.

This is why I chose women from seven different countries. This is why I included Muslim and Christian voices, war zones and corporate boardrooms, extreme poverty and middle-class stability. I wanted us to see the full spectrum. I wanted us to recognize both the universal human experience of struggle and the particular, context-specific nature of what each woman faces.

So as you read these stories, don't just extract the inspiration. Pay attention to the context. Ask yourself: What does this woman have access to that others don't? What barriers does she face that I don't? How does her context shape what "rising" even means for her?

And then ask: How can I use my context, my access, my resources, my platform, whatever privilege I have to make rising easier for women whose context is harder than mine?

Because here's the truth: If you have resources, access, education, citizenship, safety—use it. Use it not just to raise yourself, but to lift others. Use it to dismantle the barriers that shouldn't exist in the first place.

Rising is contextual. But liberation should be universal.

Rising Is a Choice—But Not Everyone Has Equal Access to That Choice

This is the hardest lesson, and the most important one to name honestly.

The title of this book is She Chose to Rise. And it's true—every woman in these pages made a choice. They chose courage over safety. They chose voice over silence. They chose to keep going when giving up would have been easier.

But let's be clear: Not every woman has the same access to that choice.

The women in this book had something—someone who believed in them, access to education, a moment of opportunity, a community that caught them, resources that created possibility. Without those things, would they have risen? Could they have?

I think about the women who don't have those things. The women who are so crushed by poverty that survival is all they can manage. The women who are trapped in abusive relationships with no way out. The women who live under regimes that will kill them for speaking. The women who are refugees with no legal status and no path forward. The women who are disabled and facing systems that were never designed for them. The women who are battling mental illness without access to care.

Are they not rising because they're not choosing to? Or are they not rising because the systems, structures, and circumstances they face make that choice nearly impossible?

I refuse to use these stories as a weapon against women who are still in their rubble. I refuse to say, "If they can do it, anyone can." Because that's not true. And it's cruel.

Yes, rising is a choice. But some women are being asked to make that choice with their hands tied behind their backs, in the dark, with no map, no resources, and no one witnessing them.

So if you are a woman who has risen, even partially, even imperfectly—recognize that you had help. You had something. Don't weaponize your rising against women who haven't had the same access.

And if you are a woman who feels like you can't rise, who feels like these stories are beautiful but impossible for you—please hear me: You are not failing. The systems are failing you. And your worth is not measured by your rising. You are valuable simply because you exist. You are worthy simply because you are human.

Rising is a choice. But justice demands that we make that choice more accessible, more possible, more supported for every woman everywhere.

This is why the work doesn't end with inspiration. It must extend to action. To policy. To systems change. To redistribution of resources and power.

Otherwise, we're just celebrating the women who had access while ignoring the women who didn't.

And that's not rising. That's privilege.

So now what?

You've read these stories. You've walked with these women through their rubble and their rebuilding. You've seen what's possible. You've felt something shift in you, maybe inspiration, maybe recognition, maybe conviction, maybe discomfort.

Now what do you do with that?

I'm going to ask you to rise. But I'm going to be specific about what that means, because "rise" is a beautiful word that can mean everything and nothing if we're not intentional.

I'm inviting you to rise on three levels: personal, communal, and systemic. All three matter. All three are necessary. None of them is sufficient alone.

Rise In Your Own Life

Start here. Start with yourself. Not because you matter more than anyone else, but because you can't give what you don't have. You can't lift others if you're not standing.

Step 1: Identify your rubble moment.

What is the thing that broke you? What is the wound you're still carrying? What is the place where you stayed down because rising felt impossible?

Name it. Write it down. Say it out loud.

Maybe it's a relationship that ended and took your sense of self with it. Maybe it's a career failure that made you believe you don't have what it takes. Maybe it's trauma from childhood that you've been trying to outrun. Maybe it's a dream you gave up on because someone told you it was impossible. Maybe it's a voice inside you that's been silent for so long you've forgotten it exists.

Name it.

Because here's what these stories teach us: You can't rise from something you won't acknowledge. The rubble doesn't disappear by ignoring it. It only becomes the foundation when you're willing to look at it, sit with it, and decide what you're going to build.

Step 2: Choose one area where you need to rise right now.

Not ten areas. One.

Rising is not about fixing everything at once. It's about choosing one thing and committing to it. Maybe it's your voice, deciding to speak up in that meeting, that relationship, that situation where you've been silent. Maybe it's your boundaries—learning to say no, to protect your energy, to stop accommodating everyone else at your own expense. Maybe it's your healing—finally getting therapy, finally addressing the addiction, finally facing the thing you've been avoiding. Maybe it's your dream—dusting it off, taking one small step toward it, refusing to let fear or practicality kill it.

Choose one thing. One area. One decision.

And then take one action toward it this week.

Not someday. This week.

Step 3: Find your community.

You cannot rise alone. I've said it before, but it bears repeating: Every woman in this book had witness. They had community. They had people who believed in them when they didn't believe in themselves.

Who is in your community? Who are the women who see you, who hold you, who remind you who you are?

If you don't have that community yet, build it. Join a book club. Find a mentor. Show up to a women's group at your church or mosque or community center. Join an online community of women doing the work you want to do. Reach out to that woman you admire and ask her to coffee.

Don't wait for community to find you. Go find it. Build it. Show up for it.

Step 4: Use your voice.

What story are you not telling because you're afraid of what people will think? What truth are you not speaking because it feels too vulnerable, too risky, too much?

Your voice matters. Your story matters. And somewhere, someone needs to hear it.

Maybe you share it in a journal first—just for you. Maybe you share it with a trusted friend. Maybe you share it more publicly—in a blog post, a social media post, a conversation at work, a testimony at church. Maybe you write it down and put it in a drawer, knowing that someday, your daughter or granddaughter will find it and understand that she comes from a line of women who refused to stay silent.

However, you share it, share it.

Because silence protects no one. Silence only protects the systems that want us quiet.

Rise For Other Women

Now let's expand the circle.

Personal rising is essential, but it's not enough. We are connected. We are communal. Your rising creates space for mine. My rising creates space for yours. And together, we create a movement.

Step 1: Witness someone else's rise.

Who is the woman in your life who is in her rubble moment right now? Who is struggling, fighting, trying to rise but not sure if she can?

See her. Really see her.

Don't try to fix her. Don't minimize her pain. Don't rush her healing. Just witness her.

Say: "I see you. I believe you. I'm here."

And then show up. Consistently. Not with grand gestures, but with presence. A text message. A phone call. Showing up at her door with food. Sitting with her in silence. Letting her cry. Celebrating her small victories. Reminding her who she is when she's forgotten.

Witness her.

Because maybe you are the person who makes her rising possible.

Step 2: Mentor, sponsor, advocate.

If you have risen in any area—career, education, leadership, healing, voice—reach back and pull someone else up.

Mentor a young woman. Sponsor a colleague. Advocate for someone who doesn't have access to the room you're in. Share your knowledge. Open doors. Make introductions. Give opportunities.

Don't wait until you've "arrived." You don't have to be perfect to help someone else rise. You just have to be a few steps ahead and willing to reach back.

Step 3: Share resources.

What do you have access to that others don't? Money? Time? Education? Networks? Platform? Citizenship? Language skills? Professional expertise?

Share it.

If you have money, invest in women-led organizations. If you have time, volunteer. If you have education, teach. If you have networks, make introductions. If you have platform, amplify other women's voices. If you have citizenship or legal status, use it to support those who don't. If you have professional expertise, offer it pro bono to women who can't afford it.

You don't have to have a lot to share. You just have to be willing to share what you have.

Step 4: Amplify voices.

The world is full of women whose stories deserve to be heard but who don't have the platform, the access, or the privilege to be heard widely.

Amplify them.

Share their work. Quote them. Tag them. Give them credit. Step aside and let them speak. Use your platform, whatever size it is—to lift voices that are marginalized, silenced, or ignored.

This is not about being a savior. This is about recognizing that some voices have been systematically silenced, and those of us with access have a responsibility to share the mic.

Rise To Change The World

Personal and communal rising is beautiful. But if we stop there, we're just putting Band-Aids on broken systems.

We need systemic change. We need to dismantle the structures that keep women down in the first place.

Step 1: Support organizations working on women's issues.

There are incredible organizations around the world fighting for women's rights, women's safety, women's economic empowerment, women's health, women's education, women's leadership.

Support them. Donate if you can. Volunteer if you can. Amplify their work. Attend their events. Sign their petitions. Show up.

(See the Resources section at the back of this book for specific organizations you can support, both globally and in the countries represented in these stories.)

Step 2: Vote with women's rights in mind.

If you live in a democracy, you have power at the ballot box. Use it.

Vote for candidates who support policies that uplift women: equal pay, reproductive rights, paid family leave, affordable childcare, healthcare access, education funding, protection from violence, pathways to citizenship for immigrant women.

And if you're not in a democracy, or if your democracy is fragile, like in some of the countries represented in this book, fight to protect it. Speak up. Organize. Resist authoritarianism in all its forms. Because when democracies fall, women are always among the first to lose their rights.

Step 3: Challenge systems that keep women down.

Where do you have influence? In your workplace? Your community? Your faith institution? Your family?

Use it.

Challenge policies that disadvantage women. Call out sexism when you see it. Push back against cultures that normalize violence, harassment, or discrimination. Advocate for change in hiring practices, promotion processes, leadership structures.

You don't have to have formal power to challenge systems. Every time you speak up, you create a crack in the system. And cracks become openings. And openings become change.

Step 4: Join the Global Rise & Soar movement.

This book is the beginning, not the end.

I am building a movement; a global community of women committed to rising together and lifting each other. A space for storytelling, for learning, for connecting, for action.

Join us.

Visit globalriseandsoar.com to:

- Share your story
- Join the conversation
- Attend events
- Access resources
- Connect with women around the world who are choosing to rise

This is bigger than a book. This is a movement. And we need you.

Let me paint you a picture of the world we are building. The world I believe is possible

It's a world where every girl grows up knowing she was created with purpose—that before she was formed in the womb, God knew her and had a calling for her life, that her voice matters, her story matters, she matters. Where she doesn't have to choose between her strength and her femininity, between being powerful and being graceful, between leading and loving. Where she sees women who look like her in positions of influence and knows, without question, that she belongs there too.

It's a world where women rise not by trying to be men or competing on men's terms, but by embracing the fullness of who we are, strong and tender, fierce and graceful, capable and compassionate. Where we understand that our strength doesn't diminish our beauty, and our beauty doesn't diminish our power. Where we honor what makes us uniquely women without apologizing for it.

It's a world where women recognize that true transformation doesn't come from systems alone—it comes from something deeper. From faith, from community, from a power greater than ourselves working through us. Where we acknowledge that when we rise, we're not rising in our own strength alone. We're being lifted. We're being held. We're being guided by something sacred.

It's a world where women support each other the way women have always supported each other in the great stories, celebrating each other's victories, mourning each other's losses, mentoring the next generation, showing up when it costs us something. Where we recognize that there's enough space for all of us to answer our callings. Where we reach back and pull each other up instead of climbing alone.

It's a world where violence against women is unthinkable because we recognize that every woman is sacred, valuable, worthy of protection and dignity. Where stalking, harassment, assault, and abuse are called what they are: evil. Where communities stand up to protect the vulnerable. Where women can walk in safety, exist in peace, and move through the world without fear.

It's a world where women's work, especially the work of raising children, building homes, and nurturing communities is honored, not diminished. Where mothers aren't punished for choosing family. Where caregiving is recognized as essential, sacred work. Where whether a woman is called to the boardroom or the living room, the mission field or the marketplace, her work matters because it's done with purpose and love. to them.

It's a world where women's voices are heard, in our communities, in our workplaces, in our homes, in the public square.

It's a world where women have equal access to education, opportunity, and resources, not because we demand it through anger alone, but because we recognize that justice requires it. Where widows are protected and provided for. Where daughters are seen as blessings, not burdens. Where women's stories are told, believed, and valued because our stories testify to resilience, faith, and the power of choosing to rise.

It's a world where women understand that we can be both grounded in faith and committed to justice. That these aren't opposites—they're partners. Where we fight for equality not to compete with men, but to partner with them in building a better world. Where we honor the beautiful ways women reflect strength, wisdom, and love. Where we seek transformation that begins in the heart and extends to systems, policies, and cultures.

It's a world where women answer their callings with confidence, whether that calling is to lead, teach, heal, build, create, serve, or nurture. Where we stop asking for permission to use the gifts we've already been given. Where we step into the assignments already written for us. Where we raise up women who will risk everything for their people, who will lead with wisdom, who will choose loyalty and courage, who will mentor and guide the next generation.

This is the world I'm building through Global Rise & Soar, a movement rooted in faith, grounded in purpose, and committed to justice. Where women rise not by tearing down men, but by building up our communities. Where we recognize that we are called to partnership, not competition. Where we honor the distinct and beautiful ways women contribute to this world. Where we seek transformation that is both spiritual and practical, both personal and systemic.

This is my commitment: I will continue to create spaces where women can discover their purpose, heal from their wounds, and step into their callings. Where faith and justice walk hand in hand. Where we rise together, believers and seekers, women from every background, every country, every story.

Because here's what I know: When women rise in the fullness of who they were created to be—strong and feminine, faithful and justice-seeking, gentle and fierce—everything changes.

Families are strengthened. Communities thrive. Nations transform. The next generation inherits a better world.

This is not just a dream. This is the work. And it begins with each woman who chooses to rise.

What will you stand up and say?

What rubble will you transform into a foundation? What silence will you break? What woman will you witness? What system will you challenge? What future will you build?

The world is waiting for your story.

The world is waiting for your voice.

The world is waiting for you to rise.

Sister, you are not alone. You have never been alone. You are part of a lineage of women who rose before you, your mother, your grandmother, your great-grandmother, women whose names you'll never know but whose strength runs through your veins.

And you are part of a community of women who are rising with you, across borders, languages, cultures, and time zones. We are here. We see you. We believe in you.

Rise, sister. Rise.

Not because it's easy. Not because you're ready. Not because you have it all figured out.

Rise because staying down is not an option. Rise because your daughters are watching. Rise because we need your voice. Rise because you were born for this.

This is your moment. This is your choice. This is your rising.

Welcome to the movement.

Welcome to Global Rise & Soar.

Welcome home.

Acknowledgments

This book exists because six remarkable women said yes when I asked them to share their most vulnerable moments with the world. Elita, Zineb, Marianna, Olga, Adelaida, and Elira, your courage humbles me. Your stories will change lives. Thank you for trusting me with your truth.

Each contributor continues to do transformative work in her community. To support their ongoing missions, please see the 'About the Contributors' section.

To my Lord and Savior Jesus Christ, thank you for blessing me with this vision and for surrounding me with the right people to bring it to life. To my foster parents, Reverend Donald Taylor and Pastor Jariatu Taylor, and my siblings, Lucy, Sarah, Ayo and David, thank you for directing me to Christ and for showing me what it means to have a family again. I still remember the day you welcomed me into your home and said, 'You're not a guest here, you're our daughter and sister.' Those words changed everything. To my mother, Khadija, who taught me that rising is not optional for women like us—it is survival. Every page of this book carries your strength.

To the organizations and institutions that invested in a girl from Freetown who dreamed of amplifying women's voices: Hope Pathways Global, Thunderbird School of Global Management, the Fulbright Program at the Walter Cronkite School of Journalism (Arizona State University) and Kansas State University, the Association of Fundraising Professionals (AFP) Arizona Chapter, BBC Media Action Sierra Leone, Engage Salone, the Mandela Washington Fellowship (YALI), Fourah Bay College (University of Sierra Leone), the 50/50 Women Group, Sierra Leone Association of Journalists (SLAJ), God-At-Work Ministry, the Sierra Leone-US Alumni Association, and the International Food Club (IFC). This is what you made possible.

To Edward Kargbo and Parul Agrawal, who read every draft at 2am and never stopped believing, Jeffry Timmermans, and Rodmanned Nikpour, whose strategic insight shaped the podcast aspect of this project from vision to reality, you believed in this project when it was just a whisper. You read drafts, asked hard questions, and reminded me why this work matters. I am because you are.

To the mentors, colleagues, and friends who have believed in my vision and invested in me over the years: Adrienne Spencer, Sonal Lal, Millicent Kargbo, Dr. Aisha Ibrahim Fofanah, Dr. Fatu Taqi, Dr. Isaac Massaquoi, Dr. Joshua Nicol, Dr. Bernadette Cole (blessed memory), Naasu Fofanah, Ariana Oluwole, Joanne Smith, Angelia Rorison, Julia Wallace, Adekalie Bangura, Nikki McClaran, Juan Mundel, Honorable Ramatulai Wurie, Haja Mariama Sesay, Kathleen Tate Mulligan, Winnie Jada, Abdul Kariim Sharief Saad, Sara Hambleton, Phebean Swill, Josephine Kamara, Eastina Massaquoi, and more—I say thank you.

To my roommates at 548—Anitah, Elita, and Ramesh, Thank you for giving me a home and a sense of family in my own little corner of the world. Thank you for your understanding, especially with the midnight podcast editing noise—and for the quiet support, including making sure I have a good meal on days I'm too exhausted to cook. Most of all, thank you for embracing our differences and the beauty of sharing cultures from different parts of the world. I couldn't have asked for it any other way.

To my faith community at The Well Phoenix, who prayed for me through Saturday evenings and beyond, thank you for reminding me that storytelling is ministry.

And to every woman who will read these stories and recognize herself, this is for you. Your rise is inevitable. We're just here to remind you.

About the Contributors

Elita Karim (Bangladesh)

Dilshad Karim Elita, known professionally as **Elita Karim**, is a celebrated Bangladeshi singer, journalist, and media innovator. As lead vocalist of the band Raaga and a solo artist, she has captivated audiences with hit songs including "Ure Jete Chai," "Nijhum Raat," "Kothay," and "Bristey." Her 2015 debut solo album *Elita* and 2024 EP *Chini Der Chamoch* showcase her commitment to authentic, melody-driven storytelling that blends contemporary Bangla pop with emotional depth.Beyond her musical career, Elita serves as Editor of Arts & Entertainment at *The Daily Star*, Bangladesh's leading English-language newspaper, where her award-winning journalism earned her the Red Cross International Award. In 2021, she was selected as a Hubert H. Humphrey Fellow at Arizona State University's Walter Cronkite School of Journalism and Mass Communication, where she met editor Mariatu Esther Kabba. Born in Saudi Arabia to a family of artists, Elita uses both her literal and metaphorical voice to amplify stories that matter—through music that moves souls and journalism that changes minds.

Zineb Haddaji (Tunisia / Djibouti)

Zineb Haddaji is a Djiboutian documentary photographer, whose work explores identity, memory, and resilience across the Horn of Africa and the wider Arab world. Her storytelling often weaves personal experience with social observation, illuminating the silent struggles shaped by beauty norms, migration, and belonging. In The Girl Who Stood Still Under the Sand, she reflects on childhood, displacement, and the long path toward self-acceptance. Born in southern Tunisia and later finding a sense of home in Djibouti, Haddaji's trajectory informs a body of work grounded in empathy and critical inquiry. She is currently a Humphrey Fellow at Arizona State University, where she continues to develop cross-cultural narratives that give voice to overlooked communities.

Elira Canga (Albania)

Elira Çanga is a journalist and communication professional, media trainer and educator from Albania. She has 20 years of experience divided between active journalism, media development and communication for international organisations. She has been working as journalist and editor for local media outlets as well as BBC in Albania. She also worked as a media expert and communication professional for international organisations as OSCE, UNICEF, World Bank and WHO. During 2022-2023, she served as a media and communication adviser to the President of Albania, planning strategically media relations and appearances as well as communication approach of the institution. She holds a Master on EU Studies and she is pursuing her PhD program at Walter Cronkite School of Journalism, Arizona State University.

Marianna Silva (Brazil)

Marianna Brandão de A. e Silva is a Brazilian business development leader and storyteller based in Arizona. Over more than a decade, she has worked in technology market development, building international partnerships across the private sector and public initiatives with a focus on growth and impact. During her Master of Global Management at Thunderbird School of Global Management, she deepened her work in sustainability and environmental solutions for innovative companies. Marianna is passionate about women's leadership, cross-cultural connections, and turning complex challenges into practical action. Her writing explores identity, courage, and the quiet strength that comes from family roots and community. She believes leadership is not only a title, but a daily choice to serve, learn, and stay open. Outside of work, she recreates Brazilian recipes as a way to honor her roots, memory, and belonging. Through business and meaningful relationships, Marianna invites others to rise with purpose and build a future that is both bold and human.

Olga (Ukraine)

Olga Usenko, Ph.D., is a Ukrainian legal media manager, analyst, and Hubert H. Humphrey Fellow at Arizona State University, specializing in strategic communications and research on Ukraine's reconstruction. For nearly two decades, she has led major analytical projects in Ukraine's legal sector. Her personal and professional journey has been deeply shaped by the war, strengthening her belief in resilience, human dignity, and quiet courage. She is committed to bringing a Ukrainian perspective to discussions on reconstruction, justice, and piece building

Dr. Adelaida V. Severson (United States)

Adelaida V. Severson, Ph.D., is President and CEO of Bushtex, Inc. She founded Bushtex, Inc. with her late husband, Barry, in 1994, as a satellite communications firm, specializing in remote broadcast transmissions worldwide. She has a diverse professional background in public relations, broadcast journalism, marketing, events management, philanthropy, and satellite communications. Additionally, she teaches courses on international communications at the university and corporate levels and is a member of the International Women's Forum (IW). Born and raised in Hawaii, Dr. Severson graduated with a B.A. in Journalism and International Relations from the University of Southern California. She received a Masters of Mass Communication and a Ph.D. in Public Administration from Arizona State University. Dr. Severson has received numerous awards and accolades with Bushtex throughout her career. She has traveled to 120 countries and is passionate about her three sons and grandchildren. She enjoys travel, music and mentoring others, especially women.

About the Editor

Mariatu Esther Kabba

Founder, Global Rise & Soar | Founder & Executive Director, Hope Pathways Global

Mariatu Esther Kabba is a storyteller, global education strategist, and advocate for women's empowerment whose work bridges Sierra Leone, the United States, and communities worldwide.

Born and raised in Sierra Leone, Mariatu's journey began with loss and displacement. When her father died at age six, she became one of millions of fatherless daughters navigating systems designed to silence women and erase their worth. From sleeping on a church floor after choosing her voice over shelter, to training hundreds of journalists across West Africa, to standing on international stages—Mariatu's story is one of relentless rising.

But this book is not just her story. It is her invitation to a movement.

Global Rise & Soar

Mariatu is the founder and visionary behind Global Rise & Soar, a global education, storytelling, and empowerment company dedicated to helping individuals, communities, and organizations unlock their potential and rise into new levels of impact.

Through digital education, book production, multimedia storytelling, strategic consulting, and transformative live experiences, Global Rise & Soar creates spaces where voices are amplified, stories become tools for transformation, and communities across the U.S., Africa, and worldwide are strengthened through connection and purpose.

She Chose to Rise is the first major initiative of Global Rise & Soar and represents Mariatu's commitment to building a global movement where women's stories are honored, their voices are heard, and their courage inspires others to rise.

What's Next for Global Rise & Soar:

- The She Chose to Rise Podcast – Intimate conversations with the women featured in this anthology and others from around the world
- Live Storytelling Events & Summits – Bringing women together across borders to share, heal, and rise
- Digital Education Programs – Leadership development, AI literacy, and digital transformation training for women and girls in underserved communities
- Future Anthology Volumes – Continuing to amplify women's stories from every corner of the globe

Learn more at globalriseandsoar.com

Hope Pathways Global Inc

As the founder and executive director of Hope Pathways Global (formerly Strong Women, Strong Girls Sierra Leone), Mariatu has spent over a decade working in media development and women's empowerment.

She has:

- Trained 200+ journalists across Sierra Leone and West Africa through the BBC Media Action Girls' Education and Empowerment Project
- Mentored young women in rural communities, creating pathways to education and leadership
- Advocated for gender equality in education, media representation, and leadership development

- Built partnerships with organizations across Africa and the United States to expand access to opportunity for girls and women

Hope Pathways Global continues to operate programs in Sierra Leone, and Arizona, providing mentorship, digital skills training, and educational support to girls who like Mariatu once was—are fighting for futures that seem impossible.

Education & Recognition

Mariatu holds a Bachelor of Arts in Mass Communications from Fourah Bay College, University of Sierra Leone, and a Master of Global Management from the Thunderbird School of Global Management at Arizona State University.

She has been recognized as:

- One of Sierra Leone's 50 Most Influential Women (2021)
- Mandela Washington Fellow – Young African Leaders Initiative (YALI), 2021
- Fulbright Hubert Humphrey Fellow – Arizona State University (Walter Cronkite School of Journalism) and Kansas State University, 2023-2024
- Mariatu will start her PhD program at the Walter Cronkite School of Journalism, ASU in the Fall of 2026

Her work has been featured in media across West Africa and the United States, and she has trained, mentored, and consulted for organizations including BBC Media Action, the U.S. Department of State, and grassroots women's organizations across multiple countries.

Her Story In This Anthology

In this anthology, Mariatu contributes "The Night I Chose My Voice" (Chapter 3), a defining moment from her larger life story. On

May 13, 2015, she made a choice that would change everything: she chose her voice over shelter, walking out into the rain with nowhere to go, nothing to her name, and only faith to guide her.

That night—sleeping on a cold church floor in Freetown—she learned that rising isn't about comfort or certainty. It's about the moment when staying small becomes more unbearable than the risk of standing tall.

But that chapter is just one moment.

Her full story, from that church floor to training hundreds of journalists, from being called "mad" like her mother to being named one of Sierra Leone's Most Influential Women, from displacement to building a global movement, will be told in her forthcoming memoir coming end of 2026

The memoir will chronicle her childhood in Kabala and Freetown, her journey through loss and displacement, her rise through media and advocacy work, the fellowships that took her from West Africa to the United States, and the vision God placed in her spirit to build Global Rise & Soar.

For updates on the memoir and Mariatu's work, visit globalriseandsoar.com or follow @globalriseandsoar on social media.

A Woman Of Faith, A Voice For The World

Mariatu's work is rooted in her Christian faith and her belief that every woman is created with purpose, power, and a story worth telling. She honors femininity as strength, partnerships (not competition) with men, and the idea that true transformation happens when women rise together.

She operates between Phoenix, Arizona and Freetown, Sierra Leone, living out her commitment to bridge continents, cultures, and communities through storytelling, education, and empowerment.

Connect With Mariatu

Website: globalriseandsoar.com
Email: info@globalriseandsoar.com
Social Media: @globalriseandsoar (Instagram, LinkedIn, Facebook)

"When women rise, the world transforms. This is not just a belief—it is the mission that drives everything I do. Through stories, education, and community, we are building a movement. And you are invited to be part of it."

— Mariatu Esther Kabba

Discussion Questions

General Questions (For the Entire Collection)

1. The title *She Chose to Rise* emphasizes choice. How does the concept of choice appear differently in each woman's story? When was choice a privilege, and when was it a survival mechanism?
2. Several women in this collection faced moments where silence felt safer than speaking. What patterns do you notice in how they broke their silence? What conditions made it possible for them to speak?
3. How do systems of oppression (patriarchy, racism, poverty, war, colonialism) appear across these different cultural contexts? What similarities surprised you?
4. Many of these women experienced "rubble moments"—times when everything they knew collapsed. How did each woman rebuild from her rubble? What resources did they draw upon?
5. Faith appears in different forms throughout the book—Christian, Muslim, spiritual. How does faith function in these stories? What role does it play in each woman's transformation?
6. The book features women from Bangladesh, Tunisia, Sierra Leone, Albania, Brazil, Ukraine, and the United States. How do cultural differences shape each woman's experience? What themes transcend culture?
7. Several contributors speak about the importance of community, solidarity, and unexpected support. Share a moment from the stories where community played a crucial role.
8. How do these stories challenge or complicate the idea of the "strong woman"? What costs do women pay for being perceived as strong?

Questions by Story

Elita - "The Day I Stopped Running"

9. Elita describes how victim-blaming kept her silent about her stalker. How does society's treatment of harassment victims contribute to their silence? What would need to change?
10. The music shop becomes both a literal and symbolic space of transformation for Elita. What role do physical spaces play in our ability to speak truth?
11. The students who defended Elita didn't know her personally. What enabled them to act? How can we create cultures where bystanders become allies?

Zineb - "The Girl Who Stood Still Under the Sand"

12. Zineb connects beauty standards to history and geography—specifically colonialism and the slave trade. How does this historical context change your understanding of "beauty standards"?
13. Reading becomes Zineb's "lifeline." What role does education and intellectual development play in resisting oppression?
14. Zineb migrates to Djibouti and finds a place where "her face was familiar." What does it mean to find home in a place where you are not considered "other"?

Mariatu - "The Night I Chose My Voice"

15. Mariatu writes: "Two days ago, I'd made a choice: speak truth or stay safe. Use my voice or keep my shelter." Have you ever faced a moment where you had to choose between comfort and your calling? What did you choose, and what were the consequences?
16. Mariatu walks out into the rain "with nowhere to go. No safety net. No plan. Only faith." What does it take to step into the unknown with nothing but faith? When was a time you took a leap of faith, even without certainty?

17. The chapter ends: "I was cold. I was scared. I was alone. But I was free." How can someone be afraid and still feel free? What kind of freedom do you think Mariatu is describing?

Elira - "Finding Freedom Through Truth"

18. Elira connects her country's freedom from communism to her personal freedom as a woman and journalist. How are political freedom and personal freedom related?
19. Elira faces discrimination when pregnant with her third child. Why do workplaces still penalize women for motherhood? What needs to change?
20. Elira insists that women shouldn't have to choose between career and family. Do you agree? What would it take for this to become reality?

Marianna - "She Chose to Rise"

21. Marianna describes becoming "what she produced." How does work culture encourage us to tie our identity to our productivity? What are the costs?
22. The cancer diagnosis forces Marianna to pause her reinvention plans. How does illness change our relationship to time, ambition, and what matters?
23. Marianna chooses to study abroad at forty after cancer treatment. What does her story reveal about age, timing, and the possibility of starting over?

Olga - "Finding Myself in a Changed World"

24. Olga describes how COVID "disappeared in a single morning" when the war began. What does this reveal about how we prioritize and respond to crises?

25. The phrase "just live your life" becomes a philosophy for Ukrainians under war. What does this phrase mean in the context of ongoing violence?
26. Olga loses relationships to propaganda, not death. How do you maintain relationships when political or moral divides seem insurmountable?

Dr. Adelaide - "Finding Success in the 'F' Word"

27. Dr. Adelaide offers five F-words: Faith, Family, Failure, Philanthropy, and Femininity. Which resonates most with you? Why?
28. Adelaide insists that women should not compete with men on men's terms. What does she mean? Do you agree?
29. Adelaide says, "One day, your life will flash before your eyes. Make sure it's worth watching." What does a "worth watching" life look like to you?

Reflection Questions for Personal Growth

30. Which woman's story resonated most deeply with you? Why?
31. What is your own "rubble moment"—a time when everything you knew collapsed? How did you rebuild?
32. The book's title suggests that rising is a choice. What is one area of your life where you need to choose to rise right now?
33. Several women in this book found their voices through unexpected means—radio, journalism, reading, migration. How have you found or are you still searching for your voice?
34. If you were to write your own chapter for this book, what would the title be?

Questions for Book Clubs and Groups

35. This book brings together women from eight different countries and cultures. What does this teach us about the universality of women's experiences? What remains unique to each context?

36. How can we, as readers and community members, support women who are in their own seasons of rising?
37. What story from this collection will stay with you? Why?
38. If you could ask one question to any of the contributors, who would it be and what would you ask?

Call to Action

39. Mariatu invites readers to become part of the Global Rise & Soar movement. What does it mean to participate in a global women's empowerment movement? How can you contribute?
40. After reading these stories, what is one concrete action you will take to support women in your community or globally?

About Global Rise & Soar

Global Rise & Soar is a global education, storytelling, and empowerment company dedicated to helping individuals, nonprofits, and communities unlock their potential and rise into new levels of impact.

Founded by Mariatu Esther Kabba, Global Rise & Soar operates at the intersection of leadership development, global empowerment, digital innovation, and narrative change—offering programs and services that uplift voices and strengthen communities in the United States, Africa, and worldwide.

Our Mission

To create transformative spaces where voices and brands are amplified, stories become tools for change, and communities are strengthened through connection, education, and purpose-driven leadership.

What We Do

Storytelling & Book Production

We develop and produce books, anthologies, and collaborative projects that elevate diverse global voices. Through professional editing, story-crafting, and multimedia production, we help individuals and organizations share their truths in ways that inspire transformation.

Digital Education & Leadership Development

We design and deliver digital learning programs in leadership, financial empowerment, career readiness, personal growth, **artificial intelligence (AI), and digital transformation**. We provide training and courses on AI and emerging technologies to individuals, companies, nonprofits, and government agencies—helping them harness innovation to strengthen their impact and expand their reach. Our programs reach youth, women, educators, and emerging leaders across borders, equipping them with the tools to thrive in a rapidly changing digital world.

TEDx-Style Talks, Conferences & Live Experiences

We create and host storytelling platforms, leadership summits, and community-centered events that bring together change-makers, inspire collective action, and amplify voices that need to be heard.

Consulting & Strategic Advisory

We partner with nonprofits, social enterprises, and community organizations to strengthen their impact through strategy development, program design, and capacity building.

Why We Exist

At its core, Global Rise & Soar exists because we believe that when individuals rise, everything changes. Families change. Communities change. Nations change.

We believe in the power of education, storytelling, leadership, and global collaboration to create generational transformation.

And we believe that every woman—regardless of where she was born, what language she speaks, or what obstacles she has faced—deserves the opportunity to rise into her full potential and soar beyond limitations.

She Chose to Rise - Our First Initiative

This book represents the beginning of the Global Rise & Soar movement. It is a testament to what becomes possible when women from across the world are given space to tell their truths, honor their journeys, and inspire others to do the same.

Through this project, we are building:

- A **podcast series** featuring conversations with the contributors
- A **live book launch event** that brings these stories to life on stage
- **Workshops and discussion guides** for book clubs, classrooms, and organizations
- **Future editions** featuring more women's voices from around the world

Join the Movement

Global Rise & Soar is more than a company—it is a community. A movement. A commitment to building a world where every woman can rise with confidence and soar with purpose.

Here's how you can get involved:

Host a Book Discussion

Use *She Chose to Rise* in your book club, classroom, church group, or organization. Download our discussion guide and facilitate conversations about courage, resilience, and transformation.

Listen to the Podcast

Hear directly from the women in this book as they share more of their stories and wisdom in intimate, powerful conversations.

Attend a Live Event

Join us for the *She Chose to Rise* book launch and other storytelling events where these voices come alive on stage.

Share Your Story

Are you a woman with a story of rising? We are building a global storytelling fellowship and would love to hear from you.

Partner With Us

Organizations, universities, and nonprofits: let's collaborate to amplify women's voices, deliver transformational education, and create meaningful impact together.

Connect With Us

Website: globalriseandsoar.com
Email: info@globalriseandsoar.com
Social Media: @GlobalRiseAndSoar

A Note from the Founder

"I created Global Rise & Soar because I believe that stories have the power to heal, transform, and liberate. This book—and everything we are building—is an invitation. An invitation to women everywhere to step into their voices, claim their stories, and rise into the fullness of who they were created to be.

Thank you for being part of this journey. Together, we rise. Together, we soar."

— **Mariatu Esther Kabba**
Founder, Global Rise & Soar
Phoenix, Arizona & Freetown, Sierra Leone

Resources For Rising

The organizations listed below represent some of the most established and enduring efforts to empower women and girls globally. This is not an exhaustive list—thousands of grassroots organizations, community groups, and regional initiatives are doing transformative work that may not appear here.

A regular updated directory of resources including country-specific organizations, crisis support services, and newly emerged grassroots movements, could be found online

Global Organizations

UN Women

The United Nations entity dedicated to gender equality and women's empowerment, working in over 100 countries.

Website: unwomen.org

Vital Voices Global Partnership

Invests in women leaders solving the world's greatest challenges through mentorship and long-term support.

Website: vitalvoices.org

Global Fund for Women

One of the world's leading foundations for gender equality, funding grassroots women's organizations globally.

Website: globalfundforwomen.org

Malala Fund

Advocates for girls' education worldwide and amplifies the voices of girls fighting for their right to learn.

Website: malala.org

Featured Country-Specific Organizations

Hope Pathways Global (Sierra Leone & United States)

Empowers women and girls through mentorship, education, digital skills training, and leadership development across Arizona and Sierra Leone.

Website: hopepathwaysglobal.org

50/50 Group of Sierra Leone (Sierra Leone)

Working for over 20 years to achieve gender parity in politics and all areas of society in Sierra Leone.

Website: fiftyfiftysierraleone.org

Ukrainian Women's Fund (Ukraine)

The only women's fund in Ukraine, providing grants, expertise, and platforms for cooperation to women's and feminist organizations since 2000.

Website: uwf.org.ua/en

BRAC (Bangladesh)

One of the world's largest NGOs, operating programs in education, healthcare, microfinance, and women's empowerment.

Website: brac.net

Instituto Maria da Penha (Brazil)

Works to prevent and combat violence against women, named after the activist whose case led to Brazil's domestic violence law.

Website: institutomariadapenha.org.br

Association Tunisienne des Femmes Démocrates (Tunisia)

A feminist organization advocating for women's rights, legal reform, and gender equality since 1989.

Website: atfd.org.tn

UN Women Albania (Albania)

Leads gender equality initiatives across Albania, focusing on women's leadership, economic empowerment, and ending gender-based violence.

Website: albania.unwomen.org

Association pour le Bien-Être Familial (Djibouti)

Promotes family well-being, reproductive health, and women's empowerment through community health programs.

Website: Available through International Planned Parenthood Federation

Crisis Support

National Domestic Violence Hotline (United States)

24/7 confidential support for anyone affected by domestic violence, dating abuse, or sexual assault. Website: thehotline.org | Hotline: 1-800-799-7233

Crisis Text Line (Global)

Free, 24/7 crisis support via text message.

Website: crisistextline.org

Text HOME to 741741 (US), 686868 (Canada), 85258 (UK)

How To Support

Donate: Financial contributions enable organizations to expand their reach and deepen their impact.

Volunteer: Many organizations offer virtual and in-person volunteer opportunities.

Advocate: Amplify women's organizations on social media and in your communities.

Partner: Explore collaboration opportunities with organizations aligned with your mission.

Stay Informed: Sign up for newsletters and follow the work of organizations you care about.

This resource list was compiled in 2025. While we have verified that all organizations listed were active and credible at the time of publication, we encourage you to visit their websites directly—or our digital resource page—for the most current information.

Your reflections

www.ingramcontent.com/pod-product-compliance
Lightning Source LLC
LaVergne TN
LVHW010929110826
845149LV00013B/2528

9781972325070